Filthy, Funny,
and Totally Offensive

Filthy, Funny, and Totally Offensive

Jokes So Dirty
Comedians and Entertainers
Only Tell Them to Each Other

**JEFFREY L. GURIAN
and TRIPP WHETSELL**

CITADEL PRESS
Kensington Publishing Corp.
www.kensingtonbooks.com

CITADEL PRESS BOOKS are published by

Kensington Publishing Corp.
850 Third Avenue
New York, NY 10022

Copyright © 2007 Jeffrey L. Gurian and Tripp Whetsell
Foreword copyright © 2007 Paul Provenza

All Kensington titles, imprints, and distributed lines are available at special quantity discounts for bulk purchases for sales promotions, premiums, fund-raising, educational, or institutional use. Special book excerpts or customized printings can also be created to fit specific needs. For details, write or phone the office of the Kensington special sales manager: Kensington Publishing Corp., 850 Third Avenue, New York, NY 10022, attn: Special Sales Department; phone 1-800-221-2647.

CITADEL PRESS and the Citadel logo are Reg. U.S. Pat. & TM Off.

First Printing: May 2007

10 9 8 7 6 5 4 3 2 1

Printed in the United States of America

Library of Congress Control Number: 2007922592

ISBN-13: 978-0-8065-2809-0
ISBN-10: 0-8065-2809-5

Foreword

A traveling salesman's car breaks down in the middle of nowhere, late at night. He walks to the nearest farmhouse miles away, knocks on the door, and the farmer answers. "Can I help you?"

"I hope so," says the salesman. "See, my car broke down and I can't get it fixed 'til the morning and I was hoping you might be able to put me up for the night."

The farmer thinks for a moment and says, "Well . . . I guess that'd be all right. . . . But we ain't got a lot of room. You'll have to share a bed with my son."

Salesman goes, "Whoa. I'm in the wrong fuckin' joke!"

That right there is a great little joke. The levels on which that joke operate are myriad. Right there in that little joke is everything you need to know about culture right now, in a perfect, hilarious little nutshell. And it's even postmodern. It's a joke, but it's also a joke about the joke. I bet you had no idea. That is because jokes are vastly underrated.

When we were making *The Aristocrats*, Penn Jillette and I decided that the late, great Jay Marshall would be the perfect performer to introduce the joke and tell the very first version heard onscreen in the film. A showbiz veteran whose career spanned numerous generations, Jay experienced firsthand that long-gone era of vaudeville circuits and Tin Pan Alley booking agents in which the joke is steeped. Jay was the perfect person to introduce that joke in the film—not only because of his intimate history with the rarified world of the joke but also because he loved jokes. He loved collecting them, and he loved telling them. Jay could tell you countless jokes on a single subject, innumerable variations on a single joke, and knew many of their origins and permutations. He was a walking encyclopedia of the performing arts and show business, and was a treasure trove of classic jokes. But Jay never referred to jokes as "jokes." He always called them "stories." As in, "Here's a cute, funny story for you . . ." I didn't know Jay very well or for very long before he took his final curtain call at the age of eighty-four, but hearing him tell "stories" was enough to make me fall in love with him and to be deeply saddened by his passing. The love and affection he had for his "stories" made my heart soar. And to hear "stories," such as the ones you will find in this book, told offhandedly by a pro with the experience and skill of Jay's, is like watching Matisse doodle while on the phone.

It's easy to think that a joke is nothing more than a disposable piece of pop culture fluff, but the art of joketelling has its roots in the rich tradition of folklore and storytelling and deserves at least as much respect. We tell them around the water cooler at the office now instead of around the campfire on a cattle drive, but wherever people gather to get a job done or to relax afterward, jokes are invariably a part of the experience. They have been a kind of social glue that has kept us surviving since the first time Homo sapiens slipped and fell off a cliff and another went to tell the others how hilarious it was when he bounced three times off the rocks below. There will be jokes going around the Internet tomorrow that have their roots in stories that go back centuries. The names, cultural references, and vernacular change, but the essence remains the same as in all storytelling throughout the ages.

Jokes are little bubbles of existentialism and mythology that run far deeper than what they appear at first glance. A great joke encapsulates the whole range of human experience in a bite-sized morsel. All our fears, insecurities, frustrations, desires, and anxieties come into play in jokes. Subversive, ironic, often usurping of language, and minimalist in structure, great jokes have surrealist streaks that make Samuel Beckett look like an overblown amateur. A well-crafted, well-told joke can be at least as elegant and rich with ideas as a great O. Henry short story. Telling a great old joke is in many ways more elegant and difficult: It took Henry several pages to lay out a punchline, whereas a good joke zeroes in on irony in a matter of seconds. Henry didn't have the chops, the pretentious windbag. Jokes are like haiku: Less is more.

Jokes can be deconstructed in the same way as any great literature. All the things that make great opera, great plays, or great poetry great are inherent in a simple, well-told joke. The best jokes rely on character, narrative, structure, suspense, catharsis, and climax. There's social comment and political content. There's the never-ending search for love. There's hope against insurmountable odds. There's the little guy fighting authority. There's man's inhumanity to man. There's man against the cosmos. There's the search for life's meaning. There's sex. Oh boy, is there sex! And here's where it gets really interesting: It never looks like any of that is going on.

A great joke is almost more about what isn't there. There's no sets, no costumes, no seventy-piece orchestra to keep you awake because it goes on and on and on. A great joke is about all of those expansive ideas and huge concepts—but all in the span of just a few seconds with just a few well-chosen words and images. And pauses. In the telling of a great joke, the pauses matter almost more than anything. The negative space is what makes a joke really great. Where the pause belongs and just precisely for how long is as mysterious as the unified field theory. No one can explain it, and it's different for everybody, but when it works, it works, and when it doesn't, it doesn't. Like jazz. It either happens or it doesn't, and no one is fooled either way. Albert Einstein couldn't figure out how the universe worked either, just that it does.

But forget everything I've just said about jokes, because it doesn't matter. Jokes don't need you to know any of this is going on. That would only get in the way of enjoying them. That's why they're so brilliant. The less you think about what's involved, the more fun you'll have. But trust me—when you laugh at the bear asking the hunter if he really comes for the hunting, the parrot in the freezer wondering what the chicken did wrong, or the kids at the breakfast table who "sure as hell don't want any fuckin' pancakes," you are enjoying genuine literature. True art. And above all, a great story.

—Paul Provenza, comedian, actor, writer,
and director and cocreator of *The Aristocrats*

Introduction

Comedians don't really tell jokes anymore—and certainly not like the filthy ones you're about to read. In these politically correct times we live in, it's almost a hanging offense to insult any ethnic group (and who doesn't miss a good Polish joke every once in a while? How did the Polack die cooking dinner? He put his nose in the microwave).

Make the mistake of telling a "sexually oriented joke" while speaking publicly, and not only do you take the chance of offending women but you also stand a good chance of losing your job, or winding up in court, depending on your position in life and how many material things you've been fortunate enough to accumulate.

Tell a gay joke, and the Gay Pride Parade will change its route to come directly past your door.

Tell a lesbian joke in the wrong part of town, and you wind up with the opportunity to live life as a eunuch, which may have worked for some guys in ancient Rome, but in 2007 USA, it doesn't quite cut it (you'll pardon the expression).

Tell an Italian joke in the wrong part of town, and not only will they stain your best shirt with Marinara sauce (or maybe even with your own DNA) but you also could wind up sleeping with the fishes.

Tell a Jewish joke, and depending on where you are, the Jewish Defense League might seriously kick your ass, or even worse, you might get sued to death by Jewish lawyers who make great white sharks look like goldfish.

Tell a Michael Jackson joke (what's black and blue and hates sex? The kid in Michael Jackson's trunk!) and you're a front-runner for crucifixion, with no trial!

Hell, political correctness is so rampant these days that you can lose your job just for telling a female coworker you'd like to make her come until she faints, or even for just showing her your cock. Life just isn't fair.

In the entertainment world of the new millennium, the classic dirty joke has been forced to go underground. And what a shame this is, because dirty jokes have been around since the dawn of man. For example, some recently discovered cave etchings in Montana reveal this joke:

Q: Why do Tumak no like having sex with buffalo?
A: Because it such a long walk around to kiss buffalo's lips.

Leave it to political correctness, and its bastard stepchild, multiculturalism, to wipe out more than 3,000 years of comedy tradition.

To that end, we felt it our moral and creative obligation to bring the dirty joke back into the public's consciousness. And who better to supply those dirty jokes than some of the funniest men and women in the United States? Break down the barriers, and let's get our sense of humor back again.

There's nothing better, or more heartwarming, than to see a room full of people of diverse ethnicities and backgrounds all laughing together at themselves, and each other, because if you can't laugh at yourself, you're taking yourself way the fuck too seriously.

If you don't believe us, just ask Lisa Lampanelli, whose entire career is based on this concept and who appears proudly in this book, with some of the most offensive jokes ever uttered.

Think of a taboo, any taboo, and chances are it'll be broken in this mind-in-the-gutter-fest guaranteed to make even *The Aristocrats* seem like wholesome family entertainment. But be forewarned: The contents of this quaint little volume are not for the faint of heart or those easily shocked. Many graphic descriptions of sex, bodily functions, and violence are presented here in the spirit of offending as many people as humanly possible.

So now that we warned you, read on, but know one thing. If you happen to read anything in this book that offends you, we want you to know, we mean every fucking word of it!

Who knows, after finishing this book, you may even become the life of the party. Or at least kicked out of it.

—Jeffrey L. Gurian and Tripp Whetsell
New York, September 2006

Read more about Jeffrey at:

www.jeffreygurian.com and
www.myspace.com/jeffreyguriancomedy

Can we tawk? *Coauthor* Jeffrey Gurian with the one and only Joan Rivers, whom he describes as "one of the nicest people I ever wrote for."

Jeffrey Gurian
Some of My Favorites That I Wrote for the Friars Roasts

About Richard Pryor, delivered by Robin Williams

I'll never forget the first time I ever met Richard Pryor. He was standing naked in the steam room, right in front of Kareem Abdul-Jabbar, and at first glance, I thought he was Jabbar's cock.

Then he said "Hello" to me, and I said to myself, "Jeez, I always heard Black guys had huge cocks, but I never knew they could speak!"

—

About Jerry Lewis

Jerry's not too smart when it comes to sex. One time, he was getting a blowjob from this chick, and he said to her, "That feels great, dear, but your teeth are a little sharp."

She said, "That's not me, shmuck. Your cock's caught in your zipper."

The name Jerry Lewis means lots of things to lots of people. To me it means the fucking summer's over.

———

About Don King
Everything about this man is phony. Don's not even really Black. He's just so full of shit, it shows through his skin.

———

About Chevy Chase
Chevy has a really small cock. When he gets a blowjob, the girl has to hold it with a roach clip. I once went out with a girl whose clitoris was bigger than Chevy's cock.

Chevy should really have been gay, 'cause he's the perfect combination of a prick and an asshole.

———

About Kelsey Grammer
At one point, Kelsey's drinking and womanizing got so bad he checked into the Betty Ford Clinic just to try and fuck Betty Ford.
And he's not particularly smart when it comes to sex. He thinks that Black men are known for having big tits.

Joan Rivers

Nobody tells you that as you get older your vagina drops. I woke up three weeks ago, looked down, and said, "Why am I wearing a bunny slipper? And why is it gray?"

———

You want to have an orgasm? You don't need a great looking stud. Just marry a rich old guy and let him take you to a fur salon and when you say, "Should I take the sable or the mink?"—and he says, "Take both"—you'll have an orgasm like you never had in your life. Your knees will be knocking for weeks.

Jeff Pirrami

A 300-pound black lady gets off work and is waiting for the bus when she feels the urge to take a huge shit. There's nowhere to go, no bathroom for miles. The black lady can't hold it in any longer, so she squats next to the bus bench and drops a mammoth, steaming dump. A minute later, the bus pulls up.

The door opens and the black lady asks, "How much?"

The bus driver says, "For you, $3. For your son, a dollar, but he's gonna have to put the cigarette out."

—

Why did the chicken cross the basketball court?

He heard the ref was blowing fouls!

—

A son goes up to his father and says, "Dad, can I have $20 for a blow job?"

The father says, "I don't know, son, are you any good?"

Jackie "the Jokeman" Martling

Harry and Charlie are swapping stories, and Harry says, "One time during the war I was captured and held for weeks without food."

Charlie says, "How could you survive without food?"

Harry says, "It wasn't easy, but I had a big meal before I was captured and learned to eat my own shit."

Charlie says, "What? That's disgusting. I don't believe you."

Harry reaches into his pants, shits in his hand, and eats it.

Charlie says, "My God. You're a freak. We can bet big money and rake in a fortune."

Harry says, "Sounds good to me. I could use the money."

The next day Charlie sets up a bet with two local gamblers. The first gambler says, "This I gotta see. Nobody can eat their own shit."

Charlie sets down a plate full of shit in front Harry. Harry looks down, gets all ready to dig in, when all of a sudden he jumps up from the table and pukes all over the two gamblers. In a rage, the gamblers beat the hell out of Harry and Charlie, take their winnings, and leave.

Charlie says, "We lost it all. Why didn't you eat the shit?"

Harry says, "There was a hair in it."

—

A guy picks up his girlfriend in his convertible and they go for a joy ride out in the country. When they're out in the middle of nowhere, they start taking off their clothes as they're driving along. They don't realize that as quickly as they're throwing their clothes into the backseat, they're blowing out of the car. All of a sudden they run out of gas. The guy turns around to get the clothes, and there's nothing there but his sneakers.

He says, "I gotta go to town to get some gas."

She says, "I'm not staying here naked. I'll go get the gas, and you stay here."

The guy figures he can't send her into town naked, so he takes one of the sneakers and he ties it to her pubic hair. She walks into town, finds a gas station, goes up to the kid pumping gas, and says, "You gotta help out my boyfriend."

He takes one look at her and says, "Listen, lady, if he's that far in, I don't think there's anything I can do for him."

Kate Mulgrew

What do you call four Mexicans in a sinking raft?
Quatro sinko.

Triumph the Insult Comic Dog
(a.k.a. Robert Smigel)

On David Spade: David Spade is a good friend of mine. He carries a Taser for protection, but he doesn't really need it. If he really wants to stun someone, all he has to say is, "I'm fucking Heather Locklear." C'mon, Tommy Lee's cock is taller than David Spade.

—

On Ben Affleck: Asking Ben Affleck about politics is like asking me about the missionary position.

—

On Vanilla Ice: His career disappeared faster than my cock in a St. Bernard.

Eric Lyden

Have you ever had your finger in your partner's ass and felt the blunt end of a turd? It really kills the moment, doesn't it? Well, I'll tell you what's kinda neat about a moment like that . . . when it's all over with and your partner says, "I have to use the bathroom," you can say "I know."

Tim Homayoon

She was so dirty I had to lick her ass to get the taste of her pussy out of my mouth.

—

Spanish women are wild in bed. When you go down on a Spanish woman, you don't come back up. They lock you down there with their thighs . . . It's called the chimichanga move. They'll put a plunger on your head. This one Spanish woman pushed my head so far down there I swear I saw one of her unborn kids waving at me.

—

Everyone told me having sex with a virgin would be the greatest. "Pop the cherry." It was the worst. All she did was complain: "Ouch it hurts, you suck . . . ouch." All right, maybe I shouldn't have done it in her ass.

Sparky Schneider

What were Jon Benét Ramsey's last words?
"Hey, you're not Santa Claus!"

Moody McCarthy

Lady goes to the doctor and says she's concerned that her vaginal lips are too big. They hang down. "Is there anything that can be done?" she asks.

The doctor says, "Sure. I've pioneered a surgery called the 'vagina tuck'—you could be my first patient."

She says, "Well, I don't want any publicity."

He assures her it'll be totally confidential. When she awakes after the surgery there are three dozen roses in her room. In a panic, she buzzes in the doctor and says, "What's with the flowers—you weren't supposed to tell anyone!"

He says, "I didn't. One dozen are from me, for being the first patient. The second dozen are from the anesthesiologist. And the last dozen are from a little boy up in the burn unit who said, 'Thanks for the new ears.'"

Baratunde

According to new research, having a planned caesarean section does not reduce a woman's risk of suffering from postnatal depression. Doctors agree the best way for women to avoid postnatal depression is to remember to take the fucking pill.

Walter Yetnikoff

Goldberg's been in the ribbon business for over thirty years, but he never got any business from this very waspy "goyishe" place. He calls Mr. Johnson and says, "How come I never got any orders from you for ribbon."

Mr. Johnson says, "I don't wanna do business with people like you."

Goldberg says, "What do you mean people like me?"

Johnson replies, "You know."

Finally Goldberg pleads, "Look, just give me a token order. I'm an old man already. Just a token order. That's all I ask."

So Johnson says, "What's a token order?"

Goldberg says, "A token order is enough ribbon that it should go from the tip of my nose, to the tip of my pecker."

Johnson says, "I know I shouldn't do this, but okay, put me down for a token order."

Two weeks later, three tractor-trailers arrive at Johnson's place filled with ribbon. Johnson calls up Goldberg insane with anger. He says, "You told me it was just a token order, from the tip of your nose to the tip of your pecker."

Goldberg says, "That's right, Mr. Johnson, but the one thing I forgot to tell you is that the tip of my pecker is in Vladivostok!"

Dave Konig

Old man walks into a confessional. He says, "Father, I'm eighty-two years old. A few nights ago, I was in a bar. I met this gorgeous twenty-two-year-old girl—beautiful eyes, long legs, and fantastic figure—just gorgeous. Well, one thing led to another, I went back to her place and we made love all night long. Then, we got up in the morning, and we made love again. Then again. I've been making love to her all week."

The priest says, "I see. Say ten Our Fathers and ten Hail Marys."

The old man says, "Well, I can't do that—I'm Jewish."

The priest says, "You're Jewish? Then what are you telling me this for?"

The old man says, "Hell—I'm telling everybody!!"

—

I just went skiing for the first time in my life. That's a stupid sport. My ski instructor told me: "You know, if you learn how to do this, it's an incredible rush—it's better than sex!" So I figure I'm way ahead of the game because apparently I ski the same way I have sex: I go straight downhill, I don't know how to turn, I keep going until I pick up a lot of speed, then I crash into things, and everybody gets upset.

Jamie DeRoy

What's the difference between pussy and parsley?
Not everybody eats parsley.

Michele Balan

In the middle of oral sex, my partner looks at me and says you smell so fresh! I looked back and said, I should, I have a woman come in twice a week!

—

At my age, oral sex is talking about it!

—

Straight people always ask the stupid question, "How'd you know you were gay."

I got tired of the routine answers, so now I say, "Well, I was going down on this woman, and it just clicked!"

—

I once dated a guy who was an English major. He was so boring I almost fell into a comma. The whole night he was propositioning me with his dangling participle.

Women don't have a phrase like, "Suck my dick." What are we going to do, have a fight and say, "lick my vagina"?

Someone would take us up on it. That's how my last relationship started! I had a fight with this guy and said, "Suck my dick."

I'm a woman, so he was staring at me and I told him I was getting it . . . it was in the mail! When I get it, he's sucking it!

Laura Slutsky

There was an elderly man who wanted to make his younger wife pregnant. So he went to the doctor to have a sperm count done. The doctor told him to take a specimen cup home, fill it, and bring it back the next day. The elderly man came back the next day, the specimen cup was empty, the lid was on it, and the doctor asked, "What was the problem?"

The elderly man replied, "Well, I tried with my right hand . . . nothing. So I tried with my left hand . . . nothing. My wife tried with her right hand . . . nothing. Her left hand . . . nothing. Her mouth . . . nothing. Then my wife's friend tried. Right hand, left hand, mouth . . . still nothing."

The doctor looked at him and said, "Wait a minute. You mean your wife's friend, too?!"

The elderly man said, "Yeah, and we still couldn't get the lid off of the specimen cup."

Steven "Spanky" McFarlin

The FDA will not approve the Morning-after Birth Control Pill because of pressure from religious groups. I think that's silly, that pill should be in stores. I'm a man, I think that pill should be at Denny's, "I'll have the Grand Slam Thank You Ma'am." They would probably make more money if they came up with a Morning-after Pill for men; it could change his blood type.

—

Is it me, or does there seem to be a lot of old people in Florida? Actually, they're not old people, they're the parents of old people.

—

You can tell a guy in Florida got lucky if he's picking blue hair out of his teeth.

—

Last time I was there I ended up with an older woman . . . a much older woman. It got kind of kinky—her walker got caught in the ceiling fan. To this day, I think I could have saved her . . . but it just felt so goddamned good.

—

Some women enjoy eye contact during oral sex on a gentleman; others say it stings.

Ross Bennett

What do anal sex and spinach have in common? Chances are if you didn't like it as a child you won't like it as an adult.

Errol Dante

Five Cubans leave Havana harbor on a raft to go to Miami. They never know when they're going to reach the United States. There's this old man crying and someone says to him, "What are you crying about?"

He says, "I'll never see the Cuban flag again."

This twenty-year-old girl says, "You want to see the Cuban flag? I have it tattooed on my ass."

So she stands up, drops her shorts, and there's the Cuban flag tattooed on her ass. The old man says, "That's wonderful. Turn around so I can say good-bye to Fidel."

Ann Anello

Did you hear that Lorena Bobbit and Monica Lewinsky are going to be opening a new hair salon?
It's called Cut and Blow.

—

An Italian woman and a Jewish woman who have been friends all their lives retire to two different assisted living facilities. The Italian woman calls the Jewish woman and says, "So how do you like it there?"

The Jewish woman says, "The food's good and I met a nice man and he comes to my room after dinner and he feels me a little on top and then we sing Jewish songs."

The Italian woman says, "No kidding. I also met a nice man. He comes to my room after dinner and he also feels me a little on top. We don't know any Jewish songs so we just fuck."

Dick Capri

An Indian immigrant walks into a doctor's office and says, "Oh, Doctor, I do not feel well. I very sick and cannot breathe."

The doctor looks at him and says, "Here's what I want you to do. Go out and get an old cigar box and shit in it. Then I want you to puke in it and piss in it. Next, take a used box of kitty litter and some rotten eggs, and dump them into the cigar box. Take the cigar box, leave it in the sun for three weeks, and then stick your face in it and take deep breaths. After you're done, I want you to come back and see me."

The Indian follows the doctor's orders, comes back for a follow up visit, and says, "Oh, Doctor, I feel much better. I'm like a new man, but I'm just curious—what was wrong with me?"

The doctor looks at him and says, "You were homesick."

—

The Three Little Pigs, Italian-Style

Once upon a time there were three little pigs. The straw pig, the stick pig, and the brick pig. One day this nasty old wolf came up to the straw pig's house and said, "I'm gonna huff and puff and blow your house down." And he did!!!

So the straw pig went running over to the stick pig's house and said, "Please let me in, the wolf just blew down my house."

So the stick pig let the straw pig in. Just then the wolf showed up and said, "I'm gonna huff and puff and blow your house down." And he did!!!

So the straw pig and the stick pig went running over to the brick pig's house and said, "Let us in, let us in, the big bad wolf just blew our houses down!"

So the brick pig let them in just as the wolf showed up. The wolf said, "I'm gonna huff and puff and blow your house down."

The straw pig and the stick pig were so scared! But the brick pig picked up the phone and made a call. A few minutes passed and then a big, black Caddy pulled up. Out stepped two massive pigs in pin-striped suits and fedora hats. These pigs went over to the wolf, grabbed him by the neck, and beat the living crap out of him. Then one of them pulled out a gun, stuck it in his mouth, and fired, killing the wolf. Then they got back into their Caddy and drove off.

The straw pig and stick pig were amazed!!! "Who the hell were those guys?" they asked.

"Those were my cousins . . . the guinea pigs."

—

A quadruple amputee is on the beach right near the water. A woman walks by and says, "Have you been hugged today?"

The quadruple amputee says, "No."

The woman gives him a big hug.

A few minutes later, another woman comes by and says, "Have you been kissed today?"

The quadruple amputee says, "No."

The woman gives him a big kiss.

A few minutes later, a third woman comes along and says, "Have you been fucked today?"

The guy says, "No."

The woman says, "Well you're about to get fucked. The tide's coming in."

Ellen Orchid

A man goes to the doctor and says, "Doc, I need a double dose of Viagra."

The doctor says, "A double dose? That's not safe, you could have side effects! Sorry, but I can't help you."

The man says, "But Doc, I've got a big weekend coming up! On Friday, I'll be seeing my girlfriend, on Saturday, I'll see my ex-wife, and on Sunday, I'll see my wife. Please help me."

The doctor says, "Well, all right. But you have to come in on Monday to see me, to make sure you're all right."

On Monday morning, the man comes into the doctor's office, with his right arm in a sling. The doctor asks him, "What on earth happened?"

The man says, "Nobody showed up!!!"

Greer Barnes

One night I was out at this bar talking to this Asian girl, but we really weren't talking that much because her English wasn't too good, and my Cantonese wasn't so sharp. Long story short, next thing I know we're at her place doin' the nasty, when she screams out something like, "See long chow a wong ho, wong ho." So I'm thinkin' who the fuck is "Wong ho"? Turns out, I had my dick in her ass!

—

The dick is funny, but there's nothing funny about the vagina. That's some serious shit. Ever see it? It's got flaps and shutters and shit. A little doorbell. [He makes a ding-dong sound.] "Can a dick come in?"

[A girl's voice answers:] "Not tonight. Go to the back door."

—

I wish I had a vagina. Just for twenty-four hours. I'd play with it. And I'm just a kid at heart, so I know I'd stick stuff in it. All my old *Star Wars* figures [then he imitates each figure, in a way that cannot be written], ending in Darth Vader asking, "What is that smell? Someone help me get this helmet off!"

Will Jordan

Everybody talks about the size of Milton Berle's penis. But I'm much more impressed with his success with women. My God, Milton Berle has had some of the most beautiful women in the world.

Shawn said to Berle, "I heard that you had an affair with Marilyn Monroe. Is that true?"

Milton said, "Yeah sure."

"My God, Marilyn Monroe," Shawn replied, "How did you do that?"

Berle answered, "It was no big deal."

Shawn said, "Tell me this much. Was it difficult?"

Berle said, "The only hard part was getting into the coffin."

—

This guy's so cheap he plays porno tapes in reverse so he can see the hooker give the money back.

He's so gross, when he leaves the men's room, he asks the attendant for a doggie bag.

Tommy Pooch

This guy marries a virgin, and on his wedding night he can't wait to fuck her. He's going crazy in bed. He can't keep his hands off her, and she's getting very nervous.

Finally she says to him, "Honey, please, I expect you to show the same manners in bed as you do at the dinner table."

The guy says, "Fine. Please pass the pussy!"

Evelyn Liu

A man took his wife to the zoo. They're in front of the gorilla cage. The guy says to his wife, "Take off your clothes and see if you can excite the gorilla."

She's like, "Are you crazy? I'm not gonna do that."

But he keeps begging and finally she agrees. She starts to undress and the gorilla starts pounding his chest and going crazy. The more she takes off, the crazier the gorilla gets. Finally, she's naked and the gorilla is going out of his mind.

The husband opens the cage door, throws her in, and says, "Try telling *him* you have a headache!!!"

Marilyn Michaels

One balmy, clear summer night, I was sitting in the backyard of my country farm home looking at the star-filled sky when I noticed what at first I thought was a comet. After a few minutes, I realized that it was not a comet, but a flying saucer.

A few minutes later, the flying saucer landed in the field behind my country farm home and lowered a ramp. Shortly, a humanlike figure wearing a space suit and helmet walked down the ramp and approached me. It had the shape of a human woman. The alien walked up to me and took off her helmet. She was as beautiful as Bo Derek in her prime. In perfect English she asked if she could come into my house. I said that would be fine.

Once inside, the space woman asked if she could remove her space suit as she was feeling very warm. Stepping out of her space suit, I noticed that she was naked and had the figure of a Playboy Playmate; except that instead of breasts, there were two perfect rectangular emeralds on her chest. Where a human would have a navel, the space woman had a magnificent red ruby.

Looking at her pelvic area, I noticed that her pubic hair was studded with magnificent diamonds, dozens of them.

I said, "Tell me something, space woman, do all the women where you come from look like you?"

She said, "Not the shicksas!!!"

Fred Travalena

In northern California, April showers are a weather condition and in Malibu it's the name of a hooker.

Ted Alexandro

I got a blow job from a girl wearing a "What Would Jesus Do" bracelet.

I was like, "Man, I have got to get back to church. Things have really changed since Christmas of '97."

Luckily, she was good. I didn't want to have to correct her. Like, "Jesus would use less teeth. Jesus would work the balls."

Dr. Victoria "Dr. Z" Zdrok

This woman Lisa is home alone and suddenly the doorbell rings. She answers it and a guy says, "Hi, I'm your husband John's friend Billy. Is John home?"

She says, "No, John went out to the store, but you're welcome to wait for him."

They sit down and after a few minutes of silence, Billy says, "Forgive me, Lisa, but I can't help noticing you have the most amazing breasts. I would give you a hundred dollars just to see one."

At first she's shocked, but then she thinks it over and figures, "A hundred bucks just to see my boob. Why not?"

So she whips out her boob and he throws a hundred bucks on the table. A minute later he says, "That was so incredible. I'm sorry, but I gotta see both of them. I'll give you another hundred if you let me see them both. She already did one, so she figured how could it hurt to show him both.

She whips them both out, and he takes a really good look. Billy leaves, and when John comes home his wife says, "Your friend Billy dropped by."

And John says, "Oh yeah? Did he leave you the $200 he owes me?"

Ellen Karis

It's so crowded in New York City and we are so used to being on top of each other that people are oblivious to it. Like the other day, I was at the gym on the floor mat doing sit-ups, and this guy plops down within a quarter inch of me and looks over and says, "Oh, am I too close?"

I say, "No, not if I'm gonna blow you."

Maureen Langan

Two gay guys want a biological baby. They masturbate into a cup and take their combined sperm to a doctor who impregnates their female friend.

Nine months later they are looking at their baby in the nursery. All the babies are crying except for theirs.

They comment to the nurse, "Wow, our baby is the most well behaved of them all."

The nurse replies, "He's quiet now, but wait until we take the pacifier out of his ass!"

———

An American Indian boy asked his father, the chief of the tribe, "Dad, why do we have such long, complicated names, while the white man has short, simple names like Bill and Bob and Tom?"

The chief replied, "Well son, our names are symbols of what we endure at a given time. Your sister was named Small Romantic Moon over the Glistening Lake because on the night she was born there was a small, romantic moon over the glistening lake. Your brother was named Galloping White Horse of the Prairie because on the day that he was born a white horse galloped across the prairie—a symbol of strength and endurance. Do you have any other questions, Little Broken Condom made in China?"

Louis Ramey

How many Jews does it take to screw in a lightbulb?
One, you anti-Semitic piece of shit!

William DeMeo

A wife tells her husband she had a dream about dicks being auctioned off. Big ones went for $10, and thick ones went for $20.

The husband says, "How about ones like mine?"

The wife says, "Those they gave away for free."

The husband said he had a dream they were auctioning off pussies.

"The pretty ones went for $500, and the tight ones went for $1,000."

She says, "And how much for the ones like mine?"

He says, "That's where they held the auction."

Jacqueline Beaulieu

There's a drunk at the end of the bar who's really sloshed, and a woman in a really low-cut dress at the other end of the bar. She's trying her best to get the bartender's attention by waving her arm wildly, and her armpit is really hairy. The drunk sees this and yells out, "Give me a drink and pour one for the ballerina at the other end of the bar."

The bartender says, "How do you know she's a ballerina?"

The drunk says, "No one else could get their leg up that high."

Sarit Catz

Guys are always complaining that once we women get married, we don't want to have sex. That's not exactly true. We didn't really want to have sex before. It's not that we don't want to have sex. We do want to have sex. It's just that we don't want to have sex with you. And before you get all lesbian fantasy, I have one word: masturbation. You guys have all kinds of terms for it: slamming the ham, stroking the salami, waxing the dolphin. We just call it . . . better than you.

Adam Ferrara

What do you call a black man flying a plane?
The pilot, you racist motherfucker.

Elaine Stritch

If ever you find yourself physically attracted to an animal, make sure it's a horse, because then when you're finished, you can get a ride home!

Mason Reese

What's the smelliest thing on the face of the earth?
An anchovy's cunt.

Helen Hong

Paul McCartney is giving a news conference and talking about his divorce from Heather Mills, and one of the reporters says, "Paul, will you ever go down on one knee again?"

Paul says, "I'd prefer if you referred to her as Heather."

—

What did the bathtub say to the toilet bowl?

I may not get as much ass as you, but I don't take no shit!

—

What do you get when you mix 500 city officials with 500 lesbians?

A thousand people who don't do dick!

Amy Anderson

There's a German guy, a French guy, and a Polish guy and they're all talking about how difficult it is to raise teenage daughters.

The German guy said, "I went into my daughter's room the other day, and I found a shot glass, and I didn't even know she drank."

The French guy said, "I went into my daughter's room the other day, and I found cigarettes, and I didn't even know that she smoked."

The Polish guy said, "I went into my daughter's room the other day, and I found a box of condoms, and I didn't even know she had a cock."

Sandra Valls

I can't fuck a skinny girl. It's like trying to fuck a bicycle.

—

What the fuck are you guys doing when you stick two fingers in a pussy, with your fingers going downward. What are you diggin' for? Change? It's a pussy, not a payphone!

If you must do the two-finger insert, at least turn it the fuck around, and do the "C'mere" motion. C'mere, c'mere. It works every time!

Malachy McCourt

As you know Catholics have confessionals. They're like little cubicles, and the priest goes into the center one and there's a room on either side of him where the sinners go to confess their sins.

And they have shutters like a speakeasy, and he goes back and forth, left to right, listening to confessions. So one day the priest is in the confession box, and a drunk staggers into the church, and goes into the confessional. It's very dark, and the priest doesn't hear anything, so after a few minutes, he knocks on the wall. The drunk says, "It's no use knocking. There's no toilet paper in this one either."

Jessica Delfino

I have a friend who nothing offends. You can do or say anything to her, and nothing bothers her. She got raped in an alley by five guys, and one of them was Mexican, and she didn't get offended.

She said, "He worked the hardest out of them all."

—

I used to date this guy in college, and he would never have sex with me, which upset me a lot, because I thought we were going to get married and everything.

So, finally one day I decided to confront him. I went to his place and knocked on the door, and said, "Listen. We've been going out now for a week, and this whole time I feel like I've been washing my ass for nothing."

—

I got a pimple on my lip-face area, it was right on the border. And it made me very nervous that it could be herpes . . . because it looked exactly like the sores on my vagina.

—

I got a fashion tip from a homeless guy. He said, "Hey, you know what would look good on you? If you wore a belt with your jeans. Now, gimme a dollar."

I felt insulted getting a fashion tip from a guy wearing a pair of garbage bag shoes—from last season—and a pair of pants. So I overreacted a little. I said, "Hey, homeless guy. You know what would look good on you? A house."

Then I took a dollar bill out of my pocket and I chewed it up and swallowed it.

—

"My Cunt"
(Song Lyrics)

I've got a hole between my legs
It makes me cry, it makes me beg
It makes me whine, sometimes there's slime
and the goddamn thing bleeds all the time
My cunt, my cunt, my cunt, it's a selfish hole!
My cunt, my cunt, my cunt, it's a selfish hole!

The space it just takes
A baby it makes
Sometimes it waits and
sometimes it aches!
It runs on dick and it likes 'em thick, so—
Be careful not to slip on that oil slick!

My cunt, my cunt, my cunt, it's a slippery hole!
My cunt, my cunt, my cunt, it's a selfish hole!

(a mouth-made oboe solo)

It needs constant attention
I don't know its dimensions,
but it's wide like a canyon once you begin your
    dissension
It's got it's own clock
It can cook you like a wok
It's got lasers and pinchers and it plays classic rock!

My cunt, my cunt, my cunt, it's a selfish hole!
My cunt, my cunt, my cunt, it's a slippery hole!
My cunt, my cunt, my cunt, it'll eat your soul whole!
My cunt, my cunt, my cunt, it's a selfish hole.

Robert Kelly

Pussy smells. Not bad like dog shit. But not awesome like pie or
cake is all I'm saying. If I had to pick something, I would have to
say feet. Pussy smells like feet. And stop spraying shit down there
like strawberry mist. 'Cause now your pussy tastes like feet and
strawberries. That's nasty. You don't see us guys dipping our balls
in peppermint before you go down there. "Hey baby, check out
these double mint twins."

———

Sex when I was younger was great. I could pump for hours on
end. Now I just lie there flopping around like a seal that was bitten
once by a great white shark.

After sex was great. I would walk around naked showing off. I
had that sexy ass dimple. I had one. Now I have eighty-seven.

After sex now is disgusting. My girl dismounts me like she is
getting off a dirty bicycle. And then she comes back in and cleans
me with a cloth like a wounded elephant.

Carol Scibelli

Harry was begging again. "Sylvia, pleeze . . . we're married twenty-five years and you've never given me a blow job."

The man had tears in his eyes. Once again the answer was, "Ugh!" Another twenty-five years pass and Harry and Sylvia are in bed after their kids threw them an elaborate fiftieth anniversary party.

Harry is feeling frisky and tries again. "Sylvia, Sweetheart, except for no blow jobs for me we've lived a good life. Come on, Sylvia—we could kick the bucket tomorrow."

"Oh, all right . . . all right . . . just once . . . but promise you won't think less of me?" Sylvia pleads. He promises over and over again that, of course, he'll still respect her. Even more . . .

Sylvia gets to it and when it's over she runs wildly into the bathroom to wash out her mouth. Harry is in ecstasy just laying back in bed. The phone rings. Harry picks up, "Helllooo," he coos and then yells to Sylvia, "Hey cocksucker, it's for you!"

Milt Moss

How do you get rid of crabs?
Marry a cocksucker who likes seafood!

—

A black guy had to have a hemorrhoid operation. They had to roll him in flour for half an hour just to find his asshole.

—

A little boy wakes up at three in the morning. He can't sleep. He goes into his parents' room, opens the door, and stands there laughing.

He goes, "How do you like that. And they're gonna spank me for sucking my thumb."

Allan Havey

A guy walks into a bar and sees a sign hanging over the bar which reads:

HAMBURGER: $1.50
CHEESEBURGER: $2.50
HAND JOB: $10.00

The guy walks up to the bar and beckons to one of the three exceptionally attractive women serving drinks to an eager-looking group of men.

"Yes?" she says. "Can I help you?"

"I was wondering," the man says, "are you the one who gives the hand jobs?"

"Yes, I am," she replies.

The guy says, "Well, wash your hands. I want a cheeseburger."

Wil Sylvince

Two gay guys are having sex. One says to the other, "I gotta go to the bathroom, so don't come till I get back."

So the first guy goes to the bathroom and when he returns, there's cum everywhere—on the walls, on the floor, the ceiling, the light fixture, everywhere.

The first gay guy says, "What happened? You promised not to come till I came back."

"I didn't come," the second gay guy says. "I just farted."

Judy Gold

Several years ago I performed for President Clinton, and I did stand-up comedy for him as well! Anyway, the Secret Service guys were so unfriendly. It was at this private residence in Miami, and while I was backstage they kept coming up to me and saying, "Don't walk over there. Don't stand here. Don't mention this . . ."

Now, I'm like a four-year-old and I hate rules. Anytime someone tells me to do something, I just want to do the opposite. Last year I was in Washington, D.C., performing for NOW, and I looked out into the audience and noticed that it was filled with hundreds of hardened feminists who've worked their entire lives for women's rights and all I wanted to do was get on stage and say, "So, I was scrubbing the toilet while my husband was fucking me up the ass, and he says to me, 'Where's my dry cleaning?'

And then he hits me and I say, 'I'm sorry. I love you. I'm nothing without you.'"

—

I'm a single mother and after spending the entire summer alone with my kids, I realized why mothers that home school their children end up drowning them.

Rick Barber

A new restaurant opened in midtown Manhattan. It was owned and operated by a very tech-savvy restaurateur who had a real operative and talking robot that tended the bar.

The robot was not only capable of knowing how to mix over 3,000 drinks, but was conversant in eight languages and in constant online contact to the greatest news organizations on the planet. His normal opening line to any patron, aside from taking the drink order, was to ask the patron their IQ. This was off-putting to some, but many were vain enough to answer the question.

One early afternoon a patron came in and ordered a martini. True to form the robot asked the vodka drinker, "Excuse me, sir. May I ask you what your IQ is?"

The patron was impressed. He responded almost too proudly, "142!" The robot immediately began to speak of history and news.

Later that afternoon, another drinker showed up at the bar and ordered, "Scotch, please."

Sensing a slight change, the robot asked again the patron's IQ. "108," he answered. The robot began to speak of the latest sports figures and the daily game scores. The scotch man was duly impressed.

Yet later that day another arrived to order a drink. "Beer," the thirsty one shouted to the shiny barman.

Of course, the usual question passed between them, but when he asked this patron his IQ, the man said, "Fuck, I don't know. I think around 82. Why?"

The robot, without a pause, shot back, "No particular reason. I was just wondering how you liked fucking your sister."

Ron Jeremy

How do you stop a dog from humping your leg?
You suck his dick!

—

What do you call the hair between your grandmother's titties?
Her pussy!

—

How come they don't teach driver's ed and sex ed on the same day in Arab countries?
Too much wear and tear on the camel!

—

What does Michael Jackson have in common with caviar?
They're both black and come on small white crackers!

—

What did the lady say to Michael Jackson at the beach?
Please move, you're in my son!

A man's in the hospital. The doctor says, "I have good news and bad news for you."

The man replies, "What's the bad news?"

The doctor says, "While you were asleep, I had to amputate both your legs?"

The guy goes, "Oh my God, what's the good news?"

The doctor says, "The guy in the bed next to you wants to buy your slippers."

Todd Barry

A pedophile is walking into the woods with a little boy. The little boy turns to him and says, "Mister, I'm scared."

The pedophile says, "You're scared? I have to walk out of here alone."

With Brooklyn's own Tony Sirico, who plays Paulie Walnuts on *The Sopranos*. "You better make me look good," were his instructions to me when I asked him to be in this book. Don't you think he looks good? *Please* say he looks good . . .

Tony "Paulie Walnuts" Sirico

What's the difference between a hobo and a homo?
A hobo has no friends, and a homo has friends up the ass.

—

A woman says to her doctor, "Doctor please kiss me."
The doctor says, "Kiss you? What are you talking about? I shouldn't even be fucking you."

Lynn Koplitz

The only time I find a little penis attractive is when it's with big balls. It's cute. It looks like it's sitting on a beanbag chair.

Julius Alvin

How can you tell that a female bartender is really pissed at you?
There's a white string hanging out of your Bloody Mary.

—

Have you heard about the newest sequel to *The Exorcist*?
A woman hires the devil to get a priest out of her son.

—

On the first day of school, the English teacher has each pupil get up in front of the class and say what they did during the summer.
The class retard says, "Last week, my daddy fell down our well."
"That's terrible," the teacher says. "Is he okay?"
"Must be," the retard says. "Yesterday, he stopped yelling for help."

—

How do you know when you've made some really bad choices in life?
The FBI shows up and starts digging up your backyard.

Eddie Sommerfield

A man says to his friend, "You know something, I think my wife died."

He goes, "What do you mean you think your wife died?"

The first guy says, "Well, I don't know. The sex is the same, but the dishes are piling up."

—

An elderly gentleman says that everyone takes him for Jesus Christ.

His friend says, "You don't look like Jesus Christ."

So the old guy knocks on the door of a whorehouse, and the madam comes to the door and says, "Jesus Christ, are you here again?"

Arj Barker

A guy moves into a remote area, and the first night he's there, there's a knock on the door. It's an old guy, maybe seventy-five with a crusty white beard. He looks like an old coal miner or something.

"Hey there, neighbor," says the old guy. "I just wanted to welcome you to the neighborhood by inviting you to a party I'm having tomorrow night. It's gonna be great. Lots a drinkin', and dancin', and fuuuuuckin'!"

"Wow, that's really nice of you!" says the new guy. "What should I wear?"

"Don't matter," says the old guy. "It's just gonna be you and me."

Patrick McMullan

How do you catch an elephant?

You dig a hole, a big hole. You put lots of ashes in it. Then you kick the elephant in the ash hole!

Tony Darrow

The Godfather calls his head man. He says, "Anthony, go in the bathroom and jerk off, and then I wanna see you."

Anthony says, "Why?"

The Godfather says, "'Cause, I told you to. Now go in there and do it."

So he goes in and does it. He comes out, he's got it in a napkin. The Godfather looks at it and says, "Good. Now go back in there and do it again."

Anthony starts to say, "But I don't understand . . ."

The Godfather says, "Just get in there and do it."

So he goes back in and he's in there for a while, and he comes back out and he's got it in a napkin.

The Godfather says, "That's good. Now go do it one more time."

He's in there twenty minutes and he finally comes out with a little drop on the napkin.

He says, "Boss, that's all I got."

The Godfather says, "Good, now drive my daughter to Brooklyn."

—

This Mafia guy dies. You know what they put on his tombstone? "What the fuck are *you* lookin' at?"

—

A guy comes home, he says, "Honey, I just bought ice cream."

She says, "Is it hard?"

He says, "It's as hard as my dick."

She says, "Okay, pour me a cup."

—

This guy goes to the proctologist. The proctologist says, "Bend over."

The guy bends over, and the doctor sees a piece of lettuce sticking out of the guy's ass. The doctor says, "My God, what happened?"

The guy says, "Please. That's only the tip of the iceberg."

—

This guy goes to the doctor and says, "Doc, I wanna be castrated."

The doctor says, "Why?"

The guy says, "What do you care? I got the money. Just do it."

So the doctor goes in and cuts off the guy's balls. The guy's coming out of the operation.

He says, "Doc, how did it go?"

The doctor says, "It went great, but while I was castrating you, I noticed you need to be circumcised."

The guy says, "*That's* the fuckin' word I was lookin' for."

—

This seventeen-year-old girl comes home to her mother and father and says she's pregnant. The father goes nuts. He says, "Son of a bitch. Who is this guy? I want him here right now. You call him up and tell him to come over."

The guy comes over. The girl is seventeen, the guy is fifty. He's driving a Rolls-Royce. He's got a $3,000 suit on. All kinds of jewelry. He walks in and says, "I'm guilty. I don't want any trouble. I'm a very, very wealthy man, and I wanna make you an offer. If it's a boy, I'll give him $5 million and one of my factories. If it's a girl, the same. If it's twins, I'll give them $5 million each, and two of my factories. But if it's a miscarriage, I don't know what to do."

The father says, "What do you mean you won't know what to do? You'll fuck her again."

Arthur Nascarella

A guy comes into the bar with an octopus. He puts the octopus on the bar and says to the bartender, "I'll bet you $100 against three shots of Johnny Walker this octopus can play any instrument you got in the bar."

The bartender says, "You're on. Put your money up." He lays out three shots of Johnny Walker and gives the octopus a harmonica. The octopus picks up the harmonica and starts to play "Danny Boy," and all the Irishmen in the bar are crying, they're pissin' wine, and they can't believe the octopus can play so good.

The bartender says, "That's amazing."

The guy drinks his three shots, picks up the octopus, and walks out the door.

The next day he comes back and says, "This time I'll bet you $200 against five shooters he plays anything you got."

The bartender says, "You got it."

He lays out five shots, the guy puts his $200 on the bar, and the bartender hands the octopus a violin. The octopus picks it up and starts playing a wild tarantella. Everybody's dancing all over the place. All the Italian people in the bar are going crazy.

The bartender says, "I can't believe this shit."

The guy drinks his five drinks, takes the octopus, and walks out. He doesn't come back for two weeks. This time he walks in and the bartender says, "I got a quart of Johnny Walker against your thousand dollars that this time he can't play what I got."

The guy says, "You're on."

He puts the octopus on the bar, and the bartender takes out a bagpipe. The octopus takes one look at the bagpipe, grabs a hold of it, starts wrestling with it, falls behind the bar, bada-boom, bada-bing, there's glasses breaking, bottles falling, they're throwing shit all over the place, the octopus is going crazy.

The bartender starts to reach for the money. The guy stops him and says, "Whoa. Not so fast. When he realizes he can't fuck it, he'll play it."

David Lappin

The teacher says, "Let's discuss what your fathers do for a living."

Mary says, "My dad is a policeman. He puts bad guys in jail."

Jack says, "My dad is a doctor. He makes all sick people better."

The teacher says, to Johnny, "John, what does your dad do?"

Johnny says, "My daddy is dead."

She says, "I'm sorry to hear that. But what did he do before he died?"

Johnny says, "He turned blue and shit on the carpet."

Sherrod Small

A woman decides that she wants to see what it's like to sleep with a black guy, so she goes to a bar in Harlem, has a few drinks, meets this black guy, and takes him home.

They start making out, she takes him in the bedroom, takes off all her clothes, and says, "Okay honey, do what you do best."

So he knocked her unconscious and stole her TV.

Iran (Blade) Barkley

This businessman was set to go away on a trip. He had a very horny wife, and he was nervous to leave her alone, so he figured he'd try to get her something to occupy her sexually while he was gone, so he wouldn't have to worry about her cheating. He goes to this sex shop to find something that will keep her satisfied. Nothing looks right. The blow-up dolls look too real, as do the regular dildos, and he's much too jealous for that. Finally, in frustration, he explains his problem to the salesman, who at first seems stumped on what to suggest, but then reluctantly tells the guy about the Voodoo Dick. He takes out an ornate wooden box from under the counter and inside is what looks like a regular dildo.

The businessman says, "Big fuckin' deal. It looks like every other dildo in the place."

The salesman says, "Wait till you see what it can do." And then he commands, "Voodoo dick, the door."

With that the voodoo dick rises out of its box, flies over to the door, and starts fucking the keyhole with such intensity that the door starts to crack. The salesman commands, "Voodoo dick, back in the box."

And the dick flies back into the box, and lays there quietly.

The businessman is astonished and says, "I'll take it."

He takes it home and demonstrates it to his wife, and tells her whenever she feels horny to just say, "Voodoo dick, my pussy," and the dick will do the rest.

The husband leaves on his trip and after about five days the wife's getting very horny. She remembers the voodoo dick, takes it out of the box, and says, "Voodoo dick, my pussy," and the voodoo dick starts fucking her like crazy. She comes once, twice, and after the third time she's exhausted, but the voodoo dick won't stop fucking her. She tries to pull it out, but it's stuck, and she's freaking out. Her husband forgot to tell her how to turn it off. She decides to go to the hospital. So she gets in the car and drives with the voodoo dick fucking her all the way over. She's driving erratically, and she comes again and swerves off the road. A cop runs over to investigate and asks how much she's been drinking. Gasping and twitching, while still being fucked, she tells the cop she wasn't drinking, but that there's a voodoo dick stuck in her pussy and it won't stop fucking her.

The cop looks her right in the eye and says, "You expect me to believe that? Voodoo dick, my ass!"

April Macie

My boyfriend asked me if I could count on my hands how many blow jobs I've given in my life to other guys.

I said, "Yeah, if I was the Hindu goddess Shiva."

—

I almost drowned today while masturbating in the bathtub. I don't have the money for a removable showerhead, so I had to use the faucet. You know where your priorities are when getting off becomes more important than breathing.

Gary Gulman

A guy walks into a pet shop and sees this parrot. The parrot sees the guy and says, "Fuck you."

The guy says, "What?"

The parrot says, "You heard me. Go fuck yourself you ugly fuck. You sicken me, you ugly piece of shit."

The guy's horrified. He runs out of the pet shop all upset. The pet shop owner comes over to the parrot, and says, "If you ever talk that way to another of my customers, I will cut your beak off and feed you to my cat."

He throws the parrot as hard as he can back into the cage. The parrot makes it quite clear he understands it's not gonna happen again. Weeks later, the same customer comes back in the store.

The parrot sees him and says, "Hey buddy."

The guy says, "What?"

The parrot says, "You know!"

Chris Barish

A guy goes into a bar and the piano player is playing the most beautiful song he ever heard. After it's over, he goes over to the piano player and compliments him on the song.

The piano player says, "Thanks. It's an original. I call it 'My Dick Gets Hard When You Stroke It Up and Down.'"

The guy is a little surprised, but doesn't say anything. The piano player says, "If you liked that song wait till you hear this one." He plays another beautiful song.

The first guy says, "That one was even more beautiful than the last one. What do you call that one?"

He says, "That one is called 'I Love it When You Lick My Balls.'"

The piano player excuses himself to go to the men's room, and when he comes back his fly is open and his dick is hanging out.

The first guy says, "Do you know your fly is open and your dick is hanging out?

The piano player says, "Know it? I wrote it!"

Brett Eidman

What's rodeo sex?

That's where you mount your girlfriend from behind, grab her hair, pull her head back, and whisper in her ear, "Your sister was better than you," and then try and hold on for eight more seconds without getting thrown off.

John Hoyt

What's the smartest thing that ever came out of a woman's mouth?

Einstein's cock!

Joe Rigano

In the last presidential election, someone asked me what I thought of John Kerry, and I used a biblical reference to give my answer. I told them, in the Garden of Eden, when God wanted to make a partner for Adam he took Adam's rib and made a woman. Five minutes later, he went to his asshole and made John Kerry.

Gregg Rogell

A couple is having sex, and the guy says, "Can you spread your legs a little wider? A little more . . . more . . . wider . . . wider . . ."

Finally, the woman says, "Jesus, are you trying get your balls in there?"

And the guy says, "No, I'm trying to get them out."

Patrice Oneal

A question Patrice likes to address to the women in his audience:

—

How would you keep your man if you didn't have a pussy?

Say there was a terrible train accident, and the doctor was like, "We gotta remove your pussy right away or you're gonna die."

How would you keep your man past the three months of like, "I can't leave the bitch, cause she just lost her pussy in a train accident."

Most women go either, "Awww, he can fuck me in the ass . . . or . . . I'll suck his dick." And then I'll go, "Look at that. I asked you what would you do to keep your man, and instead of saying I'll learn new skills, I'll learn to play X-Box, or some shit like that, you just qualified yourself as a series of holes, and I'm supposed to treat you special?"

—

Black guys need to learn some sick shit from white guys when it comes to sex. The only dirty thing I brought to sex was fish hooking. I knew about that. You're fucking your girl from the back, you reach around, put the index finger of each hand inside her cheeks and pull them apart, and she sticks her tongue out like a fucking fish.

—

Then there's "the Blumpkin," where a guy gets a blow job while he's sitting on the toilet taking a shit.

—

How about "the Omelet"?

You come in her ear and then fold it over to the other ear.

—

The Donkey Punch.

That's when you're fucking your girl from behind, and as soon as you get ready to come, you punch her in the back of her head, and her body seizes up on your dick, and it's the best nut you'll ever have.

———

Then there's "the Fish Eye," where you're fucking your girl from behind, then you pull it out, and stick the tip in her ass, and she looks back at you with one eye like, "What the fuck was that?"

———

The Chicken Cutlet

The Chicken Cutlet's nasty. It's when you're fucking your girl at the beach, you put your dick in her vagina, take it out, dip it in the sand, and you put it back in her vagina. Thus, the "parmigiana."

———

How about "Puff the Magic Dragon"?

You come in your girl's mouth. She tries to spit it out, you hold it closed, you tickle her, and it shoots out her nose.

———

The "Angry Pirate" is great. First you come in your girl's eye, then you kick her in the leg, and she hops around holding her eye and yelling "Aarrgh" like a pirate.

———

"The Houdini" is really fun though. You're fucking your girl, and just before you come you spit on her back so she thinks you came, and when she looks back, you really get her in the face.

———

"The Spider Man" . . . you come in your hand, and then you sling it in her face.

Adam Gilad

This guy crash lands on an island with Jessica Alba. They're the only two people alive on this island, and of course all he wants to do is sleep with her, but she wants nothing to do with him. He's not that attractive, and he's much older than her. So he goes out and fishes, brings her a fish, cooks it up for her, and feeds her. It's really good and she's very grateful. He builds her a shelter, so she has a place to live, and covers the floor with palm fronds, and she's very comfortable, and again is very grateful for all the care he's showing her. He builds her a hammock, and does everything he can think of to make her comfortable.

And the days pass, and the weeks pass, and he takes such good care of her that she finds herself slowly falling in love with him. So after many, many, many months, she finally starts sleeping with him. She's just so grateful to him, and one day she says, "You know, I'm so grateful to you, I'd do anything for you."

He says, "Great." So one day they're walking along the beach, and he says to her, "You said you'd do anything, right?"

And she says, "Yeah."

So he says, "I made this little sport jacket out of reeds, and seaweed. Would you mind wearing it for me?"

She thinks it's a little strange, but she agrees and puts on the sports jacket. He says, "Thank you."

The next day they're walking on the beach, and again she says, "I love you so much I'd do anything for you."

And he says, "Great. I fashioned this little moustache out of the hairs of one of the animals on the island, and I was wondering if you'd wear it for me."

She thinks it's a little strange, but she agrees, because she loves him so much, and she puts on the moustache. As usual, they make love that night. The next day they're walking along the beach, and once again she says, "I love you so much, I'd do anything for you."

She's wearing the sport jacket and the moustache, and he says to her, "There's one other thing. Can I call you Steve?"

And she looks a little confused, but she says, "That's a little weird, but okay, you can call me Steve."

And he goes, "Great! Steve, you'll never believe this, I'm fucking Jessica Alba."

Dick Lord

I'm doing a show in a hotel, and from the stage, I see a beautiful woman sitting at the bar. She's watching the show, and she seems to be enjoying herself, and I think to myself, "James Bond . . . he's almost seventy years old, and women love him. I'm like him. I'm in show business, I have a tuxedo, I speak well."

So after the show, I walk over to the woman at the bar, and I say in my best James Bond voice, "Lord, Dick Lord." And she says, "Off, . . . Fuck Off!"

Johnny Lampert

A "golf widow" concedes that if she is ever to see her husband she needs to learn the game. So she goes to the country club and signs up for lessons with the golf pro. They get out to the course and the pro instructs her to hold the club as she would her husband's cock. She hits the ball and the pro exclaims, "Beautiful!! Great shot, right down the center of the fairway!

"Now, take the club out of your mouth and we'll go for distance."

—

Sue and Dan are in their hotel room on their wedding night, preparing to consummate their marriage. Sue says, "I have one thing to tell you before we get in bed. I've had sex with one other man before I met you."

Dan thinks a minute and says, "That's no big deal. Who was it?"

Sue replies, "The famous golfer, Tiger Woods." They jump into bed and have a good session.

Afterward, Dan gets out of bed and begins to put on his underwear.

"What are you doing?" asks Sue.

"I thought I'd get dressed and fix some coffee."

Sue says, "Tiger wouldn't have done that."

"No?" says Dan. "What would Tiger have done?"

"He'd have climbed back in bed with me and done it again."

"All right!" says Dan, "Let's go." They have another pretty good session, a little longer this time. Wearily, Dan gets to his feet and begins to put on his underwear.

"What are you doing?" asks Sue.

"I thought I'd dress and get some coffee."

Sue says, "Tiger wouldn't have done that."

"No?" says Dan. "What would Tiger have done?"

"He'd have climbed back in bed with me and done it again."

Dan climbs back into bed, and this time a virtual marathon takes place. Afterward, he slinks out of bed, braces himself against the bedpost, and tries to get a leg in his underwear.

"What are you doing?" asks Sue.

"Going for a cup of coffee."

Sue says, "Tiger wouldn't have done that."

"No?" says Dan. "What would Tiger have done now?"

"He'd have climbed back in bed with me and done it again."

Dan plods to the nightstand and picks up the phone. "Who are you calling?" Sue asks.

"Tiger Woods," says Dan. "I want to find out what par is on this fuckin' hole."

Tom Fontana

Steve Allen was on a plane with Jack Benny and Jack Benny, of course, never did blue material ever in all of his career. All of his material was very funny, standard stuff. Nothing dirty. They were on a plane sitting together, when all of a sudden they see Gina Lolabrigida sitting in front of them. At the time she was considered one of the most beautiful, sexiest women in show business. Steve Allen said something to Jack Benny like, "Wouldn't you like to sleep with Gina Lolabrigida?"

And Jack Benny answered, "I want her to put my dick in her mouth, and just say her name over, and over, and over again."

Steven Garrin

I was mad at my girlfriend. She wanted a pet, so I bought her a skunk for a present.

She said, "What am I going to do with a skunk?"

I said, "I don't care . . . do whatever you want with it."

She said, "Where am I going to keep it?"

I said sarcastically, "Stick it between your legs."

She said, "What about the smell?"

I said, "Don't worry about it. He'll get used to it the same way I did."

Andy Vastola

I have great respect for women . . . sorry, I should be politically correct: Vaginal Americans.

Roger Dreyer

What did the elephant say to the naked man?

"How can you possibly breathe through that thing?"

Dante Nero

I dated a girl who weighed 512 pounds. The great thing about dating a girl that big is that no matter where you grab her on her body it still feels like a titty. I spent a lot of time suckin' on her back, and I accidentally titty-fucked her calf once.

—

Two flies are arguing on a toilet seat.

One gets pissed off!

Joseph (Joe Brat) McBratney

This woman goes to the eye doctor. She says, "I don't know what's happening, Doc. My eyes are just going on me."

So he says, "Come look at the eye chart."

He points to the second line and says, "Can you see this?"

She says, "I can't see anything."

He points to the biggest letter on top. "Can you see this?"

Again she says, "I can't see anything."

With that he whips out his dick and says, "Can you see this?"

She says, "Yes, I can see that."

The doctor says, "Just what I thought. You're cockeyed."

Joey Gay

When I masturbate at my house, it's like there's a murder going on. The doors are locked, the shades are drawn, the phone is off the hook . . . everything's wrapped in plastic.

—

I got thrown out of Starbucks last week because the guy in front of me ordered an eggnog latte. Where do you get the balls to take the two gayest substances on earth and put them in a cup? I couldn't keep my mouth shut.

I screamed out, "And stir it with a cock."

—

Do you think blind guys wanna come on their girlfriend's face?

Jordon Ferber

I was thinking the other day that the tampon is kind of like the road flare for the vagina. It's kind of like, "Warning . . . there's something on the road you may not want to see."

I drove by there, it looked kind of messy. Just be sure you have a condom handy if you wanna do any rubbernecking. That's all I'm saying.

—

A traveling salesman is going door to door. He comes to a house, Little Johnny comes to the door wearing a cape, drinking a glass of scotch, and smoking a cigar. The salesman says, "Son, is your mother home?"

Little Johnny flips up his cape, takes a swig of the scotch, flicks his ashes on the carpet, and says, "What the fuck do you think?"

Nic Novicki

This guy found out about this whorehouse that had this whore who was supposed to give the best blow job in the world and she whistles a beautiful tune while she gives it. He decides to check it out, so he goes to the whorehouse and the madam tells him that the girl he's looking for is on the third door on the left. So he goes in there and waits for the girl. Five minutes later a girl walks in the room and tells him that she is the girl that he's been looking for. She tells him that he has to first turn the light off. So he agrees and sure enough it was the best head he ever got and she whistled a beautiful tune during the blow job.

The experience was so amazing that he decided to go back and again she made him turn the light off and again it was the best head while she whistled a beautiful tune. He was determined to find out how this whore was able to give head and whistle at the same time, so he went back and positioned himself next to the light. When she was in the middle of the act, he turned the light on and on the dresser he saw a big glass eye staring at him. [Then I usually used to motion fucking the eye.]

—

I don't like lesbian porn, because there is no real ending to a scene of lesbian porn. It just keeps going and going. With a couple's scene in a porno, you've got a pretty good idea of when it's over, because after a while there's not that much left to do. Other than stand there and look awkward. But lesbian scenes just keep going and going. It's hours and hours of, "Oh yeah, oh yeah, oh yeah. [five-second pause] Yeah, yeah." I think they need to create a special ending so that people like me know it's over! Like a headbutt or something. Because blood trickling down a lesbian is usually the curtain call.

—

As a good looking little person, I get a lot of people who have fetishes. One time I got a phone call at two in the morning from this chick.

She said, "Nic do you want to come over?" Before I even answered, she hit me with the fetish. "Well, I was thinking maybe we could try something different. Maybe you can go to the store and pick up some chocolate sauce and some strawberries . . . and two more little people."

I was like, "Whoa, whoa—red flag! It's late at night, I don't know where you think I'm going to find strawberries."

Bruce Christensen

As a comedian, I am always checking out all sorts of alternative news sources to come up with fresh, interesting, original material. I want to do material that no one else is even touching on and recently I ran across this little item. Apparently, badminton is really popular around the globe. Here in the States not so much, but around the world a lot of different countries have their own badminton team. These teams all have flashy uniforms, play in leagues, and have championships, and they all have some sort of catchy name.

Does anyone here happen to know what the name of the bad-minton team from New Zealand is? You're not going to believe this. The name of the badminton team from New Zealand is . . . the

Black Cocks!!! I kid you not. When I first saw this, I didn't believe it. I thought it was one of those fake news stories, so I Googled it. I typed in "badminton, New Zealand, black cocks," enter. The search page results popped up. The first entry was from the *New Zealand Herald*, the next entry was from the *Auckland Daily News*. It turns out to be true! The name of the badminton team from New Zealand is the Black Cocks!

Well the reason why it's even making news right now is because New Zealanders in general are fed up with it. Anytime they go on vacation, or holiday, as they call it, people always come up to them and ask, "New Zealand, eh, is it true that the name of your badminton team is the Black Cocks?" Then there's the fans. They get really drunk at the matches and start yelling "Let's go Black Cocks!!!" for hours on end. Plus, all these fans went out and had T-shirts printed up, *on their own,* that say: "Black Cocks Go Harder." So New Zealanders overall are just over it all. They're sick of the jokes and the comments, so they are all voting on a referendum to change the name of the team. All this information was in this one article I had seen and the headlines that ran over this article read: NEW ZEALANDERS FIND BLACK COCKS HARD TO TAKE!

John Pinette

A guy walks into a bar and sees a monkey sitting at the bar having a drink. He sits down next to the monkey, orders a drink, and asks the bartender what's up with the monkey.

The bartender says, "Wanna see something?"

The guy says, "Yeah."

So the bartender takes out a baseball bat, hits the monkey in the head, the monkey jumps over the bar, and starts sucking the bartender's cock.

The bartender says to the guy, "You wanna try that?"

The guy says, "Sure, but do you have to hit me that hard?"

Bernadette Pauley

My husband is so cute, he's absolutely adorable. If I weren't married to him, I'd fuck him.

———

I never believed in Freud's theory of penis envy until I put the television on the other day and that TV show *The View* was on and I thought, "Oh my God, I *wish* I had a penis to shove in their mouths and shut them up," because with *that* group of broads, that's the only thing that'll work.

Johnny Podell

A guy goes into a bar and tells the bartender, "I'll bet you $500 that I can piss into this cup from across the room."

The bartender looks at the guy like he's nuts, figures he's got an easy $500, and tells the guy he's got a bet. The guy goes to the other side of the room, pulls down his fly, takes out his cock, and pisses all over the place. It goes on the bar, on the walls, on other customers . . . everywhere but the cup. He walks back to the bartender, who's laughing so hard he can hardly stand up, but manages to say, "Okay pal, pay up."

The guy gives the bartender the $500, turns around, and breaks into a grin. The bartender can't help but ask, "You just lost $500. Why are you smiling?"

The guy says, "See that guy over there. I just bet him $10,000 that I could piss all over your bar, and that you'd laugh about it!"

Bill Scheft

A guy buys a motorcycle from his cousin. He knows the motorcycle is ten years old, but it shines like it's brand new. The guy says, "How do you keep this motorcycle in such great condition?"

The cousin says, "Well, since you're buying it, I'll tell you. Every time it rains, cover the motorcycle with Vaseline. That way it will never tarnish, it will always look brand new and will last you a thousand years. Just remember, every time it rains cover the motorcycle with Vaseline."

So, the guy hops on his new bike and goes to pick up his girlfriend. They're on their way to the girlfriend's parents' house for his first dinner with the parents. Before they get there, the girlfriend says, "Look, we have a little rule in my house. Anybody who talks during dinner has to do the dishes."

The guy figures it's a little strange, but he'll go along with it. So they get to the house and walk in. There's dirty dishes on the floor. There's dirty cups and saucers hanging from the ceiling. There's bowls and plates with food caked on them. There's one entire room just filled with dirty silverware. Dishes have been wallpapered over, carpeted over. The dishes have not been done in this house since World War II. So they sit down to eat.

The guy's looking at his girlfriend, and he's real horny. He figures, hey, nobody's talking anyway, so he grabs his girlfriend, rips off her clothes, throws her on the table and in front of the mother and the father, bangs the girlfriend right on the table. Nobody says a word. So they keep eating. They have a little sponge cake, and the guy's still horny. He figures, hey, the mother looks pretty good, so he grabs her, rips off her clothes, throws her on the table and in front of the father and the girlfriend, bangs the mother right there on the table. Nobody makes a peep. Now, they're having coffee.

The guy looks out the window. He sees it's starting to rain. It's starting to rain all over his new motorcycle. The guy jumps up and says, "Hey, does anybody have any Vaseline?" And the father says, "All right, all right . . . I'll do the fucking dishes!"

Adam Hunter

I just love Asian women. One time I was fingering this Asian woman, and I pulled out a fortune!

Richard Pryor Jr.

A man is fucking this girl. It's feeling so good he's really all into it, moaning and shit, and just about ready to come. He starts to pull out when all of a sudden he feels this tremendous pulling sensation. Out he comes minus his cock.

"Where's my cock?" the man yells. "Give it back!!!! I want my cock back."

And he reaches into her wet pussy with his hands to retrieve his cock, only to pull out someone else's cock. He continues screaming for his cock and he reaches in again and pulls out yet another guy's cock . . . in frustration he screams at her, "Leper whore!!! Leper whore!!!!!!"

Dick Cavett

This lady made a bean salad for a party she was having, and she left it alone for a minute. In the meantime, her son comes in and tries to load his BB gun, but accidentally drops all the BBs into the salad. He can't pick them out fast enough, so he stirs them in. She gives her party. Later, one of the ladies calls back to say what a great party it was. She said the only problem was, "I bent down to pick up my cat, and I shot my canary."

Jeffrey Ross

Nathan Lane has a lot in common with Jerry Lewis.
Back in the seventies they both started sucking.

—

In France you're known as a genius, Jerry, but then again the French don't even know when they stink. You're like the bidet of comedy, Jerry.

—

If you Google "Jerry Lewis," you can find him on Craig's List and Schindler's List.

Chris Elliott

How do you get a gay guy to fuck a woman?
You pack her cunt with shit.

Richard Belzer
Performance at the Friars Club Roast of Jerry Lewis, June 9, 2006

Gilbert Gottfried is so cheap, the only time he puts his hand in his pocket is to scratch his balls.

—

Congratulations to Gilbert. He just scored another great gig. They're doing an animated version of the Kurt Cobain story. Gilbert will be the voice of Courtney Love's snatch.

—

Lisa Lampanelli got into trouble with the IRS last year. On her tax return, she forgot to list her occupation as "Cunt."

Paul Shaffer

I can't give you a joke for your book, because I only work blue on the dais, or occasionally after 11:30 P.M. because I know I'm gonna get bleeped. The full quote that we used to say at the *National Lampoon* when we were hanging out in the seventies, when we wanted to pay homage to that era of comedy was, "Kid, don't work blue . . . because you're bright. You don't need it." [That line could have come directly from Milton Berle's lips. As a matter of fact, I think he once actually said it to me, complete with the "kid" part.—JLG]

Steven Scott

Two guys run into each other who haven't seen each other in a long time. One became a really successful tycoon, the other guy is just struggling to get by. They run into each other in a shopping mall during Christmas, and they're both shopping for their wives.

The poor guy says, "What are you gonna buy for your wife?"

The rich guy says, "I don't know. I was thinking of getting her a Mercedes-Benz and a fur coat."

The poor guy says, "Oh my God, you're getting her both, a Mercedes and a fur coat?"

The rich guy says, "Yeah, well just in case she doesn't like the Mercedes, at least I know she'll like the fur coat."

The poor guy is astonished.

The rich guy says, "And how about you? What are you planning to get for your wife?"

The poor guy says, "Oh, I was planning on getting her a pair of slippers and a dildo."

"A pair of slippers and a dildo? That's a strange combination isn't it?"

The poor guy says, "Well, I figured this way if she doesn't like the slippers, she can go fuck herself."

—

Sol the cookie maker in Brooklyn makes these famous cookies that taste like different things. He tells his friend Abe, "Abe, you're not gonna believe this. I made a cookie that tastes like pussy. Taste one."

Abe tastes the cookie and almost gags. He says, "What are you crazy? This cookie tastes like shit."

Sol goes, "Turn it around. You have it upside down."

A little boy comes into his parents' room and sees them having sex. The next morning he goes to his mother and says, "Last night I had a nightmare and I came into your room and you were naked and jumping up and down on top of Daddy. Why were you doing that?"

And the mother thinks for a second and explains, "Well, you know Daddy's kind of fat, so I was just trying to flatten him out a little."

And the little boy says, "Well, that's not gonna work."

And the mother says, "Why not?"

And the little boy says, "'Cause every day when you go to work, the lady next door comes over and blows him back up again."

Peter Miller

A man in Alabama named Bubba is arrested for having sex with a goat.

As he's settling his bail, the chief of police says to him, "You best get yourself a good lawyer, son, 'cause having sex with a goat is serious business and you're going to trial for sure."

So Bubba goes to one lawyer, who says to him, "Sure, I know who you are. You're the fella who had sex with a goat. I gotta tell you, mister, that you're in a heap of trouble. Hell, for a case like this, I gotta charge you a $5,000 retainer and $350 an hour and there ain't no guarantee I can get you off the hook."

Bubba thinks that's a lot of money. So he goes to a second lawyer, who says to him, "Yeah, I heard about it. You're the man who had sex with the goat. That's some serious stuff in these parts. I gotta charge you a $4,000 retainer and $300 an hour to take on this case, and I can't promise you'll be acquitted."

Still too much money. Bubba decides to see a third lawyer, who says to him, "I know who you are—the one who had sex with the goat, right?"

Bubba sighs and says, "Yep, that's me."

"Well, Bubba," the third lawyer says, "I know lots of folks in this county and how they think. I can help you beat this case. In fact, I'm so sure I can help you, I ain't even gonna charge you a retainer. And I'm only gonna charge you $100 an hour."

Bubba says, "It's a deal."

A week later, the case comes to trial. The county prosecutor addresses the jury, saying, "There he sits, that man named Bubba. He is accused of the most vile and disgusting things a man is capable of: he put his penis inside a goat and had sex with it. Have you ever heard of anything more depraved? And if that wasn't bad enough, after this man ejaculated inside that goat, he made that goat lick the semen off the end of his penis!"

Bubba's lawyer jumps to his feet and says, "Your honor, I object!"

The judge bangs his gavel and says, "Objection sustained." Turning to the jury, he adds, "A good goat'll do that."

Pete Correale

There's this farmer who's down on his luck He's running out of money. He can't afford to hire people to harvest his crops. He can't afford any staff at all. So he sees this magazine advertisement where you can hire these robots and program them to do any kind of work you need. He takes his last dollars and buys twelve robots to work on his farm. They send the robots, the guy programs them to do the various jobs of harvesting crops, and after about two months of them working so hard, he's just about to see a profit, when all of a sudden a cop car pulls up.

The cop says, "Listen, we've been getting a lot of complaints from people coming down this road. Apparently, the sun is deflecting off these robots, blinding drivers as they come down this road. You have to get rid of the robots."

He says, "I can't do that. I'm finally about to start showing a profit."

So he thinks about it all night and comes up with a solution. He paints all twelve robots black. The next day, only four of them show up for work!

Greg Charles

A guy calls his boss and says, "I can't come in for work today. I'm sick."

The boss says, "How sick are you?"

The guys says, "I'm fucking my cat."

Norm Crosby

Tonto and the Lone Ranger are riding across the prairie. Suddenly, Tonto jumps off his horse, puts his ear to the ground, and says, "Buffalo come."

And the Lone Ranger says, "That's amazing. You sense that? You feel that?"

And Tonto says, "No. Ground all sticky!"

Gianni Russo

A guy from Italy takes his wife to the doctor. She hasn't been feeling too good. She comes back out, they sit in the consultation room, and the doctor says, "Your wife is fine. She just needs more attention. She needs more intercourse."

The guy gets annoyed. "You're the doctor, you do it."

The wife is gorgeous, so the doctor takes her into his private office, she gets undressed, the guy hears all this moaning coming from the room, and the guy runs in and says, "What the fuck are you doing?"

The doctor says, "We're having intercourse."

The guy says, "Oh, I'm sorry, I thought you were fucking her!"

Buddy Flip

This lady works in a sperm bank. This guy walks in, and he's got a ski mask on and has a gun.

She says, "What are you doing? This isn't that kind of bank."

He says, "Shut up you, and pick up that little vial of sperm."

So she picks up the little vial of sperm. He goes, "Now drink it."

She goes, "I'm not gonna drink it."

He's like, "Drink it, or I'll blow your fucking head off."

So she takes the cap off and drinks the vial of sperm. With that he rips off the ski mask, and it's her husband.

He says, "You see, now that's not so bad is it?"

Todd Robbins

A guy in Ireland goes up to a prostitute and asks for a blow job.

She says, "Ah laddie, it's Friday, and you know I'm Catholic, and I don't eat meat."

He says, "Don't worry about it. I'm not circumcised, so just peel back the skin and eat the cheese."

Mike Bochetti

I never wanted to have kids . . . until my sister talked me into it.

—

What's the grossest thing about eating bald pussy?
Taking off the diaper first.

Duncan Jay

Little Johnny is sitting in the classroom and the teacher asks the class to come up with a word that starts with a different letter of the alphabet. She tries to avoid picking Johnny, because she knows he'll come up with a dirty word. Finally, she gets to the letter *U* and decides it's a safe enough letter to call on Johnny.

She says, "Johnny, can you tell me a word that starts with *U*?" Johnny says, "*U*, as in urinate."

The whole class starts laughing and chanting, "Urinate, urinate, urinate."

The teacher says, "Okay smartass. Go ahead and use it in a sentence."

He stands up, looks at her, and says, "You're an eight. [Urinate.] If you had bigger tits, you'd be a ten."

Howard Siegel

A doctor is showing a potential benefactor around the hospital. She's an elderly lady, and in the course of the tour, they open a door and find a patient masturbating. The woman is obviously shocked and concerned. She asks the doctor what's the meaning of that, and the doctor thinks quickly and explains that the patient suffers from a rare condition where he has to masturbate three or four times a day or else his testicles will explode. She seems to buy it, but unfortunately about ten or fifteen minutes later they open another door and find a nurse giving another patient a blow job.

The outraged woman says, "And how do you explain that?"

Still thinking quickly, the doctor says, "Same condition, better coverage."

———

There's a penguin riding through the desert on a motorcycle who is very dehydrated because he's not used to the dryness or the hot temperature. Suddenly, he notices that his bike is leaking fluid, so he pulls into the nearest garage, and while the mechanic is looking at it, he waddles across the street. Because he's so thirsty and hot, he just slams about six vanilla ice cream cones down his beak.

When that's done, he goes back to check on his bike with the mechanic, and when he asks about it the mechanic replies, "It looks like you blew a seal."

And the penguin replies, "No, no, no, that's just the vanilla ice cream."

Ice-T

A guy and a girl are sittin' in the car, and the guy's gettin' jacked off, and he's finger-bangin' the girl. They're gettin' really hot, and the windows are steaming up.

He says to her, "You little fuckin' slut. I love you."

He says, "I feel like just taking you and rolling you over and fucking you in the ass."

She says, "Fucking me in my ass? Isn't that a little presumptuous of you?"

The guy goes, "Presumptuous? Isn't that kind of a big word for an eight-year-old?"

Pat Cooper

I got something in the mail about three days ago, it said: "To the senior citizens, how to get an erection."

They give you a patch. They say you put the patch on your ass, and three hours later you get an erection. I put on the patch, and three hours later I went back to smoking.

Gilbert Gottfried
(with Gilbert's permission, from his CD *Dirty Jokes*)

A man goes to his doctor and he says, "Doctor, I've got a really embarrassing problem. I seem to be letting off these silent farts. Oh, there goes one now. They're smelly and disgusting, and I just can't seem to control it. And they're silent. Oh, there goes two more. What's wrong with me?"

And the doctor goes, "Well first of all you're going deaf."

———

A Polish kid comes home from school. He goes, "Mom, today the teacher asked a question. I was the only kid who could answer it."

The mother says, "That's great. What was the question?"

The kid says, "Who farted?"

———

A man comes home to his wife. He goes, "Honey, pack your bags, I just won the lottery."

She goes, "What should I pack?"

He goes, "I don't care. Just pack and get the fuck out."

Alan Kirschenbaum

A woman goes to a veterinarian with a big Great Dane on a leash, and she says to the doctor, "Doctor, I have this terrible problem. Every time I turn my back on the dog, he mounts me."

The doctor says, "Well, I could castrate him for you."

And she says, "No, that's not necessary. I just want you to clip his nails."

Vincent Pastore

A man goes to the doctor. He says, "My wife either has AIDS or Alzheimer's. I don't know what to do."

The doctor says, "Bring her deep into the woods and leave her there. If she finds her way home, don't fuck her."

Frank Chindamo

Several men are in the locker room of a golf club, ALL Naked, AND sweaty. A cell phone on a bench rings and a man engages the hands free speaker-function and begins to talk. Everyone else in the room stops to listen.

MAN: "Hello."

WOMAN: "Honey, it's me. Are you at the club?"

MAN: "Yes."

WOMAN: "Honey, I'm at the mall now and found this beautiful mink coat. It's only $5,000. Is it okay if I buy it?"

MAN: "Wait a minute, is this—"

WOMAN: "Honey, you let me get this coat and I will blow you like a Caribbean hurricane."

MAN: "Sure, go ahead if you like it that much."

WOMAN: "I also stopped by the Mercedes dealership and saw the newest model. I saw one I really liked."

MAN: "I don't think—"

WOMAN: "Just think of how good I'd look in the backseat of that thing. Naked. With you on top of me."

MAN: "How much?"

WOMAN: "$90,000."

MAN: "Go for it. But for that price I want it with all the options."

WOMAN: "Great! Oh, and one more thing . . . The house I wanted last year is back on the market. They're asking $950,000."

MAN: "Look, this really isn't—"

WOMAN: "I'll let you bang me in the ass."

MAN: "Ah, um, go ahead and give them an offer of $900,000. They'll probably take it. If not, we can get the extra fifty thousand."

WOMAN: "Okay. I'll see you later! I love you so much!"

MAN: "Oh I love you, too."

The man hangs up. The other men in the locker room are staring at him in astonishment, mouths agape.

He asks: "Anyone know who this phone belongs to?"

John (Cha-Cha) Ciarcia

An attractive young woman was in the doctor's office.
He said, "I'll be doing a vaginal examination now."
She said, "Oh, doctor, is that really necessary?"
He said, "Listen, who's the chiropractor here, you or me?"

Felicia Collins

This guy gets a bear hunting kit for his birthday, and he's so
excited about trying it out, he can't wait to go bear hunting. So he
goes out to the woods, and he's got his outfit on, he's got the gun
with the scope, and he's so excited, and he's looking through the
scope, when suddenly he feels a tap on his shoulder.

He turns around and it's this huge bear, and it's growling at
him. The guy is so scared he shits in his pants.

And the bear goes, "You come up here trying to hunt me, man.
You're trying to shoot me?"

And the guy is crying, "I'm sorry, I'm sorry, Mr. Bear. Please
don't kill me. I'll do anything you want. Just please don't kill me."

So the bear says, "All right. You don't want me to kill you? Then
you have to let me fuck you in your ass, and then I'll let you go."

The guy is scared shitless, but he has no choice but to agree. So
the bear fucks him in the ass, with his huge bear cock, tosses him
away, and bounds off into the woods.

The hunter is laying there, all humiliated and shit, and he's
pissed.

He's like "No bear is gonna fuck me in the ass and get away with
it." So the next night, he's back in the woods looking for the bear.

He's looking through the scope, and suddenly feels a tap on his
shoulder. It's the bear again, and this time the bear is really mad.

The bear says, "You don't give up, do you? You're still trying to
shoot me, aren't you, motherfucker?"

The hunter starts crying, "No Mr. Bear, I swear I'm not trying to
kill you."

The bear's like, "Bullshit. I know why you're here. You wanna kill me, so now I'm gonna kill you."

The hunter begs for his life again, and this time the bear says, "Okay, okay, I'll consider sparing your life again, but if you want me to let you go again, this time you have to suck my big bear dick."

The guy's like "Oh shit," but he has no choice, so he gets down on his knees, and sucks the bear's cock, and it's huge, and he dislocates his jaw, and the bear's balls hit him in the eye and give him two black eyes, and the bear finally comes in his mouth, and stalks off into the woods.

The guy is a mess. He's laying there with two black eyes, a dislocated jaw, he got fucked in the ass, and he's covered in bear cum, and he's pissed.

He's like "No fuckin' bear is gonna do that to me and get away with it. I'm gonna kill that fuckin' bear."

So he follows the bear's path, and he's laying there with his last ounce of strength, looking through the scope, waiting to shoot this fucking bear, when suddenly out of nowhere he feels this tap on his shoulder.

In horror, he turns around, and the bear is standing there with his hands on his hips, and in a very gay voice, the bear says, "Now tell me the truth. You didn't really come up here to hunt, did you???"

Susie Essman

On the Jerry Stiller Roast, which is what got me the part of Susie Greene on *Curb Your Enthusiasm*, Maury Povich was on the dais, and I looked over at him and said: "You know, Maury, we always wondered why you married Connie Chung, and then we realized: ALL Jews love to eat Chinese. Every Sunday."

Freddie Roman

A husband brings home a dozen roses for his wife.
She says, "What did you do wrong?"

He says, "Nothing. I wanted to bring you a gift, and this is how you act?"

She says, "Sure, now you want me to lie in bed naked all week with my legs apart."

He says, "Whattsa matter, you don't have a vase?"

Macio

A guy walks into a sex shop and asks the clerk to see all the blow up dolls.

The sales clerk asks the man which kind of blow up doll he's looking for.

"I'm not sure," the man replies.

"Well, let's see. We have Black, White, Asian, skinny, fat, hairy, big butts . . . but may I suggest the Arab one?" the clerk says.

With a perplexed look on his face, the man says, "An Arab one?"

The clerk says, "Yes, it's our best seller—because the Arab one blows itself up."

Russ Meneve

A guy comes home to his house with a duck under his arm, and his wife is there . . .

He says, "This is the pig I've been fucking."

His wife says, "That's no pig, it's a duck."

The guy says, "I'm not talkin' to you."

—

Did you ever get that letter from Social Security telling you what your benefits will be when you retire based on your current income? I opened mine, and there was a picture of me in bifocals blowing some guy for the rent.

Ivy Supersonic

God wants to take a vacation, but he's not sure where he wants to go. One of the Angels suggests Earth.

God thinks it over and says, "I don't know. Earth's okay, but 2000 years ago I went down there and fucked some Jewish chick, and they're still talking about it."

Joe Amiel

There was this hospital, but it wasn't a normal kind of hospital. In this hospital the nurses used to fuck the male patients to get them better. But there was this one guy who nobody wanted to fuck, because written on his thing was the word "Shorty."

So one day, one of the nurses said, "I'm gonna go in and get him better."

The other nurses said, "What are you crazy, he's got 'Shorty' written on his thing. You'll embarrass him."

She says, "I don't care."

So she goes into the room. The next morning she comes out, and all the other nurses go running over to her. They go, "What happened?"

She goes, "Girls, this was the most fantastic, the most amazing, most incredible lover you could ever ask for. It was unbelievable."

They're like, "What do you mean? He had 'Shorty' written on his thing."

She goes, "Yeah, but when it got hard it said, 'Shorty's Pizzeria, we specialize in outgoing orders, the number in New York is (212) 247-8487.'"

Vince Curatola

This couple Angela and Tony have a restaurant. Angela works in back, and Tony works out front. A blind guy walks in and asks

Coauthor Jeffrey Gurian with Vince Curatola, who plays mob boss Johnny Sack on *The Sopranos*, disguised as a doctor 'cause he's "on the lam." Actually, they're on the set of Jeffrey's award-winning short film I Am Woody, in which Vince played an M.D.

if they have a menu in Braille. Tony says they don't, but he'll be more than happy to read to him from the menu.

The guy says, "That won't be necessary. If you just bring out some of the used utensils from the kitchen, I have a really strong sense of smell, and I can identify the food I want by doing that."

Tony says, "Really?"

The guy says, "Yeah, I do that all the time."

So Tony brings out the utensils, and the guy smells them, and he says, "Okay, let's see . . . we got linguini with clam sauce, spaghetti and meatballs, and mussels marinara. That sounds good. I'll have that."

The next week the same thing happens. The blind guy comes in, asks to smell the utensils, Tony brings them out, and the guy orders his food. After a couple of weeks of this same thing happening, Tony decides to test the guy. He goes into the kitchen and tells Angela, "Ang, I got this blind guy out there, and I don't know if he's putting me on or what. Do me a favor and take this spoon, stick it inside your underwear, rub it between your legs, put it inside of you, and let's see if this guy's on the level."

So Tony brings out the spoon, along with the other utensils. The guy smells them and says, "Okay, we got fettuccine alfredo, we got penne a la vodka," and then he stops at the last one, thinks for a minute, and says, "Hey, I didn't know Angela worked here!"

Ralph Revello

A little old lady is walking down the street dragging two plastic garbage bags with her, one in each hand. There's a hole in one of the bags, and every once in a while a $20 bill falls out of it onto the pavement.

Noticing this, a policeman stops her. "Ma'am, there are $20 bills falling out of that bag."

"Damn!" says the little old lady. "I'd better go back and see if I can still find some. Thanks for the warning!"

"Well, now, not so fast," says the cop. "How did you get all that money? Did you steal it?"

"Oh, no," says the little old lady. "You see, my backyard backs up to the parking lot of the football stadium. Each time there's a game, a lot of fans come and pee in the bushes, right into my flower beds! So, I go and stand behind the bushes with a big hedge clipper, and each time someone sticks his little thingie through the bushes, I say, '$20 or off it comes!'"

"Hey, not a bad idea!" laughs the cop. "Okay, good luck! By the way, what's in the other bag?"

"Well," says the little old lady, "not all of them pay up!!!"

Daniella Rich

Don't you hate it when you're giving some guy a blow job and he just won't come, and you're humming, and whistling, and singing, and it's getting late, and you know you have to get back to your desk 'cause your boss is calling you. Don't you just hate that?

—

I don't like anal sex. I don't even like a finger back there. If I'm having anal sex, the guy better have a dick like a thermometer . . . thin, smooth as glass, and covered in Vaseline.

—

Speaking of Vaseline, one night I had on so much lip gloss, I went to blow this guy, and he slipped out of my mouth and flew into the next room.

Dave Rosner

You know those kids today who are born-again virgins?

They've sworn off sex, but do oral and anal. They've got more STDs than a full-time crack whore.

Artie Lange

A kid walks into the bathroom and catches his father putting on a rubber.

The kid says, "What are you gonna do with that, Dad?"

The father says, "I'm trying to catch a mouse."

The kid says, "Whattaya gonna do when you catch it, fuck it to death?"

Jackie Mason

A ninety-year-old man goes to the doctor with a drip. The doctor says, "Have you been with a woman recently?"

The old man says, "Yes."

The doctor says, "How long ago?"

The old guy says, "About three weeks."

The doctor says, "Do you remember her name?"

The old guy says, "Yes."

The doctor says, "Do you remember where she lives?"

Again, the old guy says, "Yes."

The doctor says, "Well you better hurry back there. You're coming."

Richard Johnson

A guy goes to work on a sheep farm in Montana, and after a few weeks he starts getting horny, but there are no women around at all. After a few more weeks he's ready to bust, and he says to one of the guys, "What do you guys do for sex around here if there are no women?"

The guy tells him to pick out a sheep, take it out into the woods, and do his thing. That's the only choice they have. So he tries to put it off as long as he can, but one day he can't take it anymore, so he picks out one of the sheep, goes out into the woods, and does his thing.

When he comes back, all the rest of the guys are laughing hysterically.

He asked his friend who told him to take the sheep why they were laughing. His friend says, "We're laughing at your taste. Of all the sheep to pick, you picked the ugliest one!"

Dave Mordal

My girlfriend recently had her clitoris pierced. It looks kind of strange, and I've chipped three teeth, but at least now I can find it every time.

—

I don't know how anyone can watch child porn. The acting is atrocious. Although the crying seems genuine.

—

I've never found glow-in-the-dark condoms useful. I know where my dick is. What I could use is a glow-in-the-dark vagina. That way I don't have to constantly hear, "Where are you trying to put that, you moron?"

Scott Baio

A guy is talking to his buddy and says, "I made a Freudian slip last week that was so bad."

The other guy says, "What did you do?"

The first guy says, "I was in line for a ticket at the airport, and the ticket agent was this gorgeous blonde with the biggest set of tits I ever saw. I couldn't take my eyes off them."

The second guy says, "And?"

The first guy says, "So when it came my turn, I accidentally asked her for 'two pickets to Tittsburgh.' Can you believe that? I was so embarrassed."

So his friend says, "Wow, that's quite an embarrassing Freudian slip, but I can actually top that. I was sitting at the breakfast table with my wife one morning, and I meant to say, 'Honey, can you please pass the sugar,' but what came out was, 'You fucking bitch, you ruined my whole life.'"

Joey Reynolds

What is a four-letter word that begins with *C*, ends with *T*, and describes a Jewish wife?

C-A-N'-T.

Goumba Johnny

A man is in an elevator with a woman. He says to her, "Excuse me, miss, can I smell your pussy?"

She says, "Absolutely not."

He says, "Oh then, it must be your feet!"

Frankie Pace

The doorbell rings to a whorehouse. A madam answers the door, but doesn't see anyone around. A voice says. "Hey, babe, got anybody decent that I can fuck?"

Looking down she sees a man with no arms and legs. She says, "How can you fuck anyone with no arms and legs?"

The man smiles and says, "Hey, I rang the fucking doorbell, didn't I?"

———

Two black guys are drunk, and they decide to take a leak off a bridge they're standing on. They pull their dicks out and get ready to piss when the first one says, "Man this water is cold."

The second guy goes, "Yeah and it's deep, too."

Mario Macaluso

A woman shopping in a pet store is being harassed by a parrot. Every time she walks by, the parrot says, "You got a hot pussy, honey, suck my big dick."

The woman is very upset and tries to ignore the parrot, but the parrot doesn't stop. Every time she walks by, the parrot says, "You got a hot pussy, honey, suck my big dick."

After the third time, the woman starts screaming at the owner that she's calling the ASPCA and having the bird put to sleep. The owner begs her for another chance and promises that the bird will never say anything like that to her again.

The next day she comes back to the store and the bird is just staring at her with a vengeance.

Finally, she says to the bird, "What?"

The parrot says, "You know."

Dan Naturman

A pedophile is driving a car. He sees a handsome young boy, pulls up, and says to the kid, "If you get in the car, I'll give you a piece of candy."

The kid says, "If you give me the whole bag, you can come in my face."

Tom Shillue

Guy goes into a confessional, kneels down, and says, "Bless me, Father, for I have sinned."

The priest says, "Will you tell me your sins, boy?"

The guy says, "Father, I had sex with a woman."

The priest begins to talk and the guy cuts him off and says, "Father, I'm not finished yet. I had sex with a married woman."

The priest says, "Oh my boy, that's bad. Will you tell me who it is?"

The guy says, "No, Father, I can't."

The priest says, "Well then, I can't give you absolution if you won't tell me."

The guy's like, "Sorry, Father, I just can't tell."

The priest says, "Tell me her name. Was it that Sharon O'Sullivan woman up the road?"

The guy says, "Father, I'm sorry, I just can't tell you."

The priest, even more frustrated, continues to question him, and says, "I know. It was Evelyn Curran wasn't it? That Curran woman who lives up by the cemetery, wasn't it?"

The guy says again, "I'm sorry, Father, but I can't tell you."

The priest, losing his patience screams, "I know who it was. It was that Mrs. Lefave, wasn't it? Mrs. Lefave, right?"

The guy insists he can't tell, and the priest throws him out of the confessional. The guy goes back into the street and his friend says, "Well did you receive absolution?"

The guys goes, "No, but I got three pretty hot leads!"

Rich Vos

A little girl goes with her father to get her first haircut. He takes her to a barber shop, sits her in the chair, and the barber puts on the smock, while she's eating a Fig Newton. The guy starts cutting her hair, and suddenly she drops the cookie. He picks it up and gives it back to her, and she starts crying hysterically.

He's like, "What's the matter, honey, you have hair on your cookie?"

She says, "What are you out of your fucking mind . . . I'm only six!"

Countess LuAnn

Why don't condoms come in black?
Because they make you look too thin.

Denise Rich

A spaceship makes a crash landing on Earth, and this space alien couple is onboard. They realize they can't stay on the ship, and they have to find a place to spend the night. They see a farmhouse in the distance, so they go and knock on the door, and a couple answers the door. They explain their situation and ask if they can possibly stay for the night.

The Earth couple figures, "What the heck, we never met any space aliens before." So they agree.

The space alien guy and the Earth guy wind up alone in the living room, and the alien asks the Earth guy, "Have you ever done it with a space alien?"

And he says, "No. Have you ever done it with a human?"

The alien says, "No." So the alien says, "Wanna switch?"

And the Earth guy says, "Sure. Let's ask the girls."

So they go into the kitchen and ask the girls, and they both agree. So the human guy goes off with the space alien woman, and the space alien guy goes off with the Earth woman. The space alien gets undressed, and the Earth woman is shocked to see how small his penis is.

He tells her not to worry. "Just pull on my ears vertically and see what happens."

So she pulls his ears up and down, and his penis gets bigger and bigger.

He tells her, "Stop pulling when you're happy with it."

She says, "That's great, but it's so thin."

He says, "Now pull my ears horizontally and see what happens."

So she pulls his ears out to the side, and it gets thicker and thicker. He says, "Stop when you're happy."

The next morning the alien couple leaves, and they all wish each other well. The Earth woman is having breakfast with her husband. She's ecstatically happy, but the husband looks very depressed. He's just staring down in to his plate.

He says to his wife, "How was it for you?"

She says, "It was amazing, unbelievable, just the most incredible sex. And how was it for you?"

The husband says, "To tell you the truth, it was the worst experience I ever had. The sex itself wasn't bad, but just when I thought it was going good, she almost ripped my ears off."

Geno Bisconte

Everyone is so afraid to say anything for fear of being perceived as a racist, which is ridiculous. Racism shows more in what we do. For example, James Earl Ray was a racist. He killed Martin Luther King just because he was black. And it was the second he pulled the trigger that he became a racist. It wouldn't have mattered if that bullet had missed and hit a murderer or a rapist, which could have easily happened. There were black people all over that rally.

Bobby Funaro

There once was a young man named Skinner,
Who took a young lady to dinner.
At a half past nine,
they sat down to dine.
By a quarter to ten he was in her.

Eddie Brill

A teacher is teaching her young class about anatomy. The teacher draws an arm on the board and asks if anyone knows what that is.

A little girl raises her hand and says, "That's an arm and my mommy has two of them!"

"Very good," says the teacher.

Now she draws a leg on the board.

A little boy raises his hand and says, "That's a leg and my daddy has two of them."

"Correct!" says the teacher. Now she draws a breast on the board. Another little girl yells out, "That's a breast and my mommy has two of them."

"What a bright bunch of children," exclaims the teacher.

Now she draws a penis on the board. A little boy blurts out, "That is a penis! And my daddy has two of them!"

"Two of them?" shrieked the teacher.

"Yes, he has a small one for peeing and a big one for brushing mommy's teeth!"

Jesse Nash

A husband and wife are lying in bed. The husband is reading the paper and keeps sticking his fingers up his wife's pussy. After a few minutes of this, the wife finally says, "Honey, if you want to make love, just tell me."

And the husband replies, "No thanks, honey, I just need help turning the pages."

—

This Englishman meets this guy from Nashville over tea in London. The Englishman, with his thick British accent, starts to explain to this southern gentleman that there are three types of teas he likes to serve each day: "Around 7:30 in the a.m., I like to serve my morning tea, which is 90 percent aromatic and 10 percent body. Around midday, I like to serve my afternoon tea, which is 90 percent body and 10 percent aromatic. And around 7:30 in the p.m., I like to serve my evening tea, which is 100 percent body."

Well, the guy from Nashville is so impressed with the British gentleman's explanation of his three teas that he decides to offer his own. In a very thick southern accent, he begins to explain the three types of teas he likes to serve when he's home in Nashville: "Around 7:30 in the a.m., I like to serve my morning tea, which is f-a-r-t, 90 percent aromatic and 10 percent body. Around midday, I like to serve my afternoon tea, which is s-h-i-t, 90 percent body and 10 percent aromatic. And around 7:30 in the p.m., I like to serve my evening tea, and that's c-u-n-t, and, of course, this "T" is 100 percent body . . . just how most of us like it!"

Bethenny Frankel

What's the biggest difference between pussy and sushi?
The rice.

—

What's the difference between eating pussy and driving in the fog?
Driving in the fog you can just about see that asshole in front of you.

—

A girl goes to her gynecologist and says, "Doctor, please help me, my pussy smells so bad that I'm losing all my friends and no one wants to talk to me."

He says to her, "You must be exaggerating. It can't be that bad. Girls always exaggerate about things like that."

So he sends her inside to take off her clothes and tells her he'll be in in a minute. He finally comes in, opens her legs, takes a sniff, and abruptly leaves the room. Five minutes later he comes back in carrying a six-foot pole with a hook on the end of it. She gets real nervous and says, "What are you going to do with that? You're not going to shove that up my pussy are you?"

"No, I'm gonna open up a couple of windows. It fucking stinks in here."

—

This young guy gets sent to jail. He's only a kid, and he's real nervous because everyone's telling him what can happen in jail. He's scared to death. He gets brought down to his cell and everyone is out working. He's wondering who he's going to be rooming with. He looks at his walls and its all pix of naked men. Suddenly, a huge black guy walks into his cell and introduces himself as Bubba.

He says, "Around here, we like to play games."

The kid is like, "Okay."

Bubba says, "I like to play mommies and daddies."

The kid says, "Okay, but I wanna be the daddy."

Bubba says, "No problem. Come on over here and suck mamma's dick."

John Femia

A guy walks into the clinic and says to the doctor, "Doc, you're the fourth doctor I've seen and I want some answers now! I'm tired of feeling bad and nobody seems to be able to help me."

"Whoa, whoa, Mr. Johnson," says the doctor. "You should have seen us first. We have the finest technology around here. We'll tell you your exact problem; all you need to do is give us a urine sample, we put the sample into the computer, and it'll give the exact diagnosis."

Mr. Johnson says, "What? You're telling me that if I give you a urine sample, you can give me the exact diagnosis of my problem?"

"That's right, Mr. Johnson," says the doctor.

So the patient provides a urine sample, the doctor puts it into the computer, and in a couple of seconds, "Beep," a sheet of paper comes out.

"Hmmm, says right here you have tennis elbow. Now, I want you to rest your arm, take these pills, and come back in two weeks with another urine sample in this cup."

Well, Mr. Johnson decides he doesn't trust this doctor either, so he gets a plan to fake him out. Two weeks go by. He takes the cup and urinates in it. He gives it to his wife, and she urinates in the cup. Then he gives it to his daughter, and she urinates in it. He then goes out to the garage and drains a little oil from his car into the cup. To add a final touch, he then masturbates into the cup. Mr. Johnson returns to the doctor's office with the "sample" and the doctor puts it into the computer. It takes five minutes to compute this answer. Finally, "Beep," the sheet of paper pops out.

"Damn, Mr. Johnson, I've got some awful news! Looks like your wife's pregnant, your daughter's sleeping with everyone in town, your Toyota needs a tune-up, and if you don't stop jerking off, you'll *never* get rid of that tennis elbow!"

———

A doctor just finishes his checkup with a man. The doctor says, "I've got good news and bad news. Which do you want to hear first?"

The patient says, "The bad news, I guess."

The doctor says, "Well, you only have about three months to live and there's nothing else we can do. I'm sorry."

The patient says, "Oh my God, my wife, my kids," and starts

crying. The doctor says, "Hey wait a minute, you haven't heard the good news yet!"

The patient says, "You just said I had three months to live. What could possibly be good news after *that?*"

The doctor leans toward the patient in confidence and says, "Well . . . you know that hot nurse I have out front?"

The patient thinks a minute and says, "Yes?"

The doctor says, "The one with the big breasts?"

The patient says more excitedly, "Yes?"

The doctor continues, "The one that always smiles and flirts with you every time you come in for a checkup?"

The patient excitedly says, "Yes, *yes*!!! What about her?"

The doctor smiles, leans over, and says, "I finally fucked her last night!"

Vinny Parco

Two gay guys are standing on the corner when a gorgeous girl walks by.

One gay guy looks at the other and says, "You know, it's times like this that I wish I was a lesbian."

———

This hillbilly chick goes to her father and asks to borrow the pickup truck. The father says okay, but only if she sucks his dick. She really wants the truck, so she starts sucking his dick, and all of a sudden she stops and says, "Your dick tastes like shit."

The father says, "Oh jeez, I forgot, your brother borrowed the truck an hour ago."

Marty Richards

A little old Jewish guy retires to Florida and buys a condominium. They tell him he can park there and to find a spot for himself.

He's driving all around, and can't seem to find anywhere to park. Finally, he sees a perfect spot and pulls in. Suddenly, he sees a gorgeous young woman waving to him from her terrace.

He looks at her and says, "Me?"

She nods "yes" and says, "Come on up."

So he goes up to her apartment, and she invites him in. She's wearing a sheer negligee, and she's absolutely gorgeous. She takes him into the bedroom and says to him, "Now pull down your pants."

He nervously he pulls down his pants.

Then she says, "Now take out your penis."

He says, "Really? You really want me to take out my penis?"

She nods "yes," so he takes out his penis. She holds out the palm of her hand and says, "Now put it right here, right in the center of my hand."

So he takes it and lays it across the center of her palm. Immediately, she takes her other hand and starts spanking it while saying, "You will never park in my parking spot again, got it?!"

George Sarris

A kid asks his father, "What's the difference between actual and theoretical?"

The father says, "You wanna know the difference between actual and theoretical? Go ask your mother and your sister if they'd sleep with someone for a million dollars."

The kid comes back a few days later and says, "They both said yes. They'd sleep with someone for a million dollars."

So the father says, "You see that's a perfect example of what you asked about. Theoretically, we have the opportunity to make $2 million, but actually we're just living with a couple of whores."

Joe Franklin

This gentleman and his wife are stranded late at night in Florida, so they go to a motel and ask if they have any rooms.

The clerk says, "Yes, sir, we have many rooms available," and he asks him to sign the register. The man writes in Mr. and Mrs. Rosenblatt. The clerk takes one look at the name and immediately says, "I'm sorry, sir, I made a mistake, we don't have any rooms available."

The guy said, "Well, you just told me you had plenty of rooms available."

The clerk said, "I must have looked at the wrong sheet. I'm sorry, but we don't have any rooms."

The man says, "Are you trying to tell me that this is a restricted hotel because my name is Rosenblatt?"

The clerk says, "No, no, no, sir, we are definitely not a restricted hotel."

The guy says, "Well, whether you are or not it's a moot point, because I'm not Jewish."

The clerk says, "You're not Jewish? What are you then?"

The guy says, "I'm Quaker."

The clerk says, "If you're a Quaker, then prove it to me."

The guy says, "Okay. Fuck Thee."

———

Three little old ladies are sitting on a park bench when all of a sudden a guy with a huge erection flashes them. The first old lady was so stunned, she had a stroke. The second old lady was equally stunned, and she had a stroke. The third old lady was too weak and frail, so the other two had to help her to reach out and have a stroke.

Jessica Kirson

So my mother is a therapist. I always go to her for comfort. I called her and said, "Mom, I have to go to the gynecologist, but I'm nervous."

She says, "Go to someone nurturing and gentle."

I'm like what is that? A nurturing gynecologist? I walk in, spread my legs, and he sings, "Look at the little vagina, look at the little vagina. Hush little pussy don't say a word. The nipples on the breasts go round and round."

Dr. Judy Kuriansky

This little old lady had a female parrot, and she was very upset because the parrot sat in its cage all day, and said, "I'm a red hot mama, and I'm ready to fuck."

She was particularly upset because she was a very pious woman, so she took the parrot to the church and told the priest, who said to her, "Don't worry. I have two male parrots in the back of the rectory, and all they do is sit all day and play with the rosary beads. They'll be perfect company for your female parrot."

So she brings in the female parrot and sets it by the male parrots who are, as usual, busy playing with the rosary beads.

The female parrot says, "I'm a red hot mama, and I'm ready to fuck."

Both male parrots drop the rosary beads, and one looks at the other and says, "Thank God, our prayers have finally been answered."

—

This man and woman are having sex for the first time. He takes off his shoes, and she notices that he has no toes.

He explains it by saying, "When I was a little boy, I had toe-berculosis."

Then he takes off his shirt, and his back is all scarred up. He explains it by saying that when he was a little boy, he had "back-teria."

Then he takes off his pants, and the woman says, "Don't tell me . . . small cox."

Kent Emmons

Queen Elizabeth is on the *Sixty-Four-Thousand-Dollar Pyramid* on Celebrity Royalty Week, and she's in the final round. Nipsey Russell is her celebrity partner across the way. Nipsey is the one giving her clues, and Dick Clark says, "And go!"

The first phrase pops up there and reads, "Horse's cock."

So Nipsey starts to laugh a little bit, and he's trying to give her a little hint, and he starts to say, "Well, it's a . . . well, it's a . . ." and he can't come up with anything to say.

Finally, the queen looks over at him and says, "Let me guess. Is it something I could put in my mouth?"

And Nipsey thinks it over, starts to laugh, and says, "Well, I guess you could put it in your mouth."

And the queen thinks for a minute and says, "By any chance, could it be a horse's cock?"

———

This man and woman are redoing their house. He sends his wife to the hardware store to get a hinge. She goes down to the store and describes the hinge just like her husband told her. The clerk goes into the back, comes out with the hinge, and says, "Okay lady, do you wanna screw for that?"

She says, "No, but I'd blow you for that clock radio up there."

———

This man is in this bar, and he's had a horrible day. He lost a ton in the stock market, his girlfriend broke up with him, and he's really, really drunk. He goes into the men's room to take a leak, when this ugly midget walks in, stands next to him, and starts taking a leak as well. He looks down, sees this ugly midget, and figures it just goes along with the rest of his day. The midget looks up at him and tells the guy he's not a midget, he's a leprechaun, it's his lucky day, and to prove it he'll give the guy three wishes.

He says, "Make a wish."

So the guy says, "You know, I've always wanted to have a really

———

nice car." The leprechaun says, "Poof. You've got a Ferrari waiting out there for you in the parking lot. What's your second wish?"

The guy says, "That's amazing. For my second wish, I need a hot blonde, 'cause my girlfriend just broke up with me."

The leprechaun says, "No problem. Poof. The blonde's waiting for you out in the car in the parking lot. What's your third wish?"

The guy is totally amazed. He says, "My third wish? I need a lot of money. I had a really bad day in the stock market, and I need a couple of million dollars."

The leprechaun says, "Is that all? No problem. Poof. The money is in the glove compartment of the Ferrari, with the blonde in the parking lot."

The guy says, "Jeez, I don't know how I can thank you. I was having such a horrible day, with the stock market losses and my girlfriend leaving me and all I don't know what to do to make it up to you."

And the leprechaun says, "Well, there is one thing you can do for me. If you want your wishes to come true, you have to let me have my way with you."

The guy says, "What?"

The leprechaun says, "Otherwise, your wishes all go away."

The guy thinks it over and says, "Of all the luck I have to meet a gay leprechaun."

But he decides it's worth it, so he says okay. The leprechaun takes him into a stall, pulls down his pants, and this leprechaun has a twelve-inch dick. He starts fucking this guy in the ass every which way but Sunday, and while he's doing the guy he starts asking him questions. "What's your name?"

The guy squeezes out the word, "Michael."

"And how old are you, Michael?"

The guy can barely speak, but he manages to say, "Forty-two."

The leprechaun laughs and says, "Forty-two, huh? A little old to be believing in leprechauns, don't you think?"

Leo Allen

A guy goes to the doctor for a checkup. The doctor looks him over, and then says, "It doesn't look good. I'm going to have to run some tests. I'm going to need a sample of your blood, a sample of your urine, and a sample of your stool."

The guy goes, "Here, just take my underwear."

Wendy Diamond

A dentist noticed that his next patient, an elderly lady, was looking very nervous, so he decided to tell her a little joke as he put on his gloves. "Do you know how they make these gloves?" he asked.

"No, I don't," she replied.

"Well," he spoofed, "there's a building in China with a big tank of latex. Workers of all hand sizes walk up to the tank, dip in their hands, let them dry, then peel off the gloves and throw them into boxes of the right size."

She didn't crack a smile.

"Oh well, I tried," he thought.

But five minutes later, during a delicate portion of the dental procedure, she burst out laughing.

"What's so funny?" he asked.

"I was just picturing how condoms are made!" she said.

Tonia Madenford

Little Red Riding Hood went hopping through the woods, and along came the Big Bad Wolf, who said, "Hey babe, I want to have crazy sex with you and fuck you doggy style." Little Red Riding Hood turned and said, "No way man, you have to *eat me*, just like the book says!"

Jay Leslie

A guy has three beautiful daughters who all have dates on the same night. The first guy arrives and says, "Hi, my name's Lou. I'm here to pick up Sue. We're going to bowl a game or two. How do you do?"

The father calls for Sue upstairs and says her date has arrived.

The second guy arrives and says, "Hi, my name's Teddy. I'm here to pick up Betty. We're going out to eat spaghetti. Is she ready?"

Again, the father calls upstairs and informs Betty that her date has arrived.

The third guy arrives, rings the doorbell, sees the father, and says: "Hi! My name's Chuck!"

And the father shoots him.

Alan Zweibel
With a Story About Jackie Vernon, from the Friars Roast for Sid Caesar

Jackie gets up and tells about a moment in Sid's life with a woman named Loretta whose dream in life was to sleep with Sid Caesar. And every once in a while Jackie would look over at Sid Caesar and say, "You remember Loretta, don't you, Sid?"

But Loretta had heard of Sid's huge, enormous member, how big and thick his cock was, and how he had worn out so many women, and she was worried that she would not be able to accommodate Sid's size.

"You remember when Loretta was so worried about pleasing you, don't you, Sid?" So the big night came, and Loretta called her mother and said, "'This is it. This is the night I think I'm going to be able to fuck Sid Caesar, but I'm nervous. I don't want him to hurt me, and I don't want to disappoint.' You remember this night, don't you, Sid?"

So Loretta's mother said, "'This is what you do, 'cause I'm very proud of you that you're going to get the chance to fuck Sid Caesar.

Go to the butcher store and buy some fresh liver. Start making out with Sid Caesar, keep the lights off, and when he's ready to take your panties off, excuse yourself for a minute to go to the ladies room, and while you're in there, put the liver between your legs, keep the lights out, and he'll never know the difference.' You remember this night, don't you, Sid? You don't mind me telling this story, do you, Sid?"

So anyway, the night comes, and they get together, and they're making out, and first the blouse comes off, and the bra comes off, and he's just about ready to take her panties off, when she remembers what her mother told her. She says, "'I'll be right back, Sid. I have to go to the ladies' room.'"

So she goes inside, takes the liver, puts it between her legs, comes back to bed, and they make love and it's amazing. Sid can't believe it. He goes once, and immediately he's ready to go again. And it's that way all night long. He never had sex like that in his life. The earth moved, and it was pure ecstasy. And Loretta was satisfied, because she was satisfying Sid. "You remember how happy she was, don't you, Sid?" After five or six times, Sid was never more ecstatic in his whole life, and had never been more sexually satisfied. He finally fell asleep in Loretta's arms. "You remember falling asleep in Loretta's arms, don't you, Sid?"

The next morning, Sid woke up and Loretta was still asleep. He didn't want to disturb her before he left, so he got dressed, and he felt so much love for her he wrote her a note, and at that moment Jackie Vernon takes a piece of paper out from his pocket and reads:

"Dear Loretta, last night was the most wonderful night of my life. I knew that I liked you, but now after making love with you, I know I'll never be the same. No other women mean anything to me. You are the new high-water mark in lovemaking for me. Never before have I experienced such passion for a woman, had so much fun, and felt so much love for anyone, so Loretta, until we meet again, I just wanted to tell you, I love you, and I can't wait until we are together again. P.S. Your cunt is in the sink!"

Julius R. Nasso

An older, white-haired man walked into a jewelry store one Friday evening with a beautiful young gal at his side. He told the jeweler he was looking for a special ring for his girlfriend. The jeweler looked through his stock and brought out a $5,000 ring and showed it to him.

The old man said, "I don't think you understand, I want something very special." At that statement, the jeweler went to his special stock and brought another ring over.

"Here's a stunning ring at only $40,000," the jeweler said.

The young lady's eyes sparkled, and her whole body trembled with excitement. Seeing this, the old man said, "We'll take it." The jeweler asked how payment would be made, and the old man stated, by check. He said, "I know you need to make sure my check is good, so I'll write it now and you can call the bank Monday to verify the funds and I'll pick the ring up Monday afternoon."

Monday morning, a very teed-off jeweler phoned the old man. "There's no money in that account."

"I know," said the old man, "but can you imagine the weekend I had?"

Larry Amoros

This guy meets a woman, they go back to his place, and he gets her into bed. She says, "Put in a couple of fingers."

So he does.

She says, "Put in a couple of more fingers."

So he does.

She says, "Put in the whole hand."

He does.

Then she says, "Now, take your other hand and put in a couple of fingers."

He does.

She says, "Now put in the rest of your other hand."

He does.

She says, "Now clap."

He says, "I can't."

She's like, "Tight, huh?"

Jeff Garlin

A comic comes offstage and this beautiful blonde comes up to him and says, "I saw you perform on Saturday night, and I think you are so amazing. I want to fuck you and do every wild thing you can think of. I want to fulfill your every fantasy."

And the comic says, "Did you see the early show or the late show?"

Paul Borghese

A guy goes home to his wife and tells her that he found a $50 bill. She asks him to give it to her for groceries.

He holds the bill up in his hand and says, "You see this bill, it's

With Jeff Garlin from *Curb Your Enthusiasm*. Jeff Garlin and Jeff Gurian. If not for three letters, you'd never be able to tell us apart.

mine." He then holds it up to a mirror and says, "You see that bill [pointing to its reflection in the mirror], that one's yours."

She says, "Okay."

Next day he comes home and there are all kinds of different meats all over the table for dinner, a feast. Everywhere he looks is food. He asks, "Where did all the meat come from, honey, you know we can't afford this?"

She walks over to the same mirror and holds up her dress. Pointing to the reflection of her vagina in the mirror, she says, "You see that, that's yours."

She then points to it away from the reflection and says, "You see this, this is the butcher's."

Ann Lee

I don't care much for feng shui. However, I do practice the art of fuck shui.

Aleta St. James

A journalist went to visit a woman who was diagnosed with a fatal disease and had only been given a year to live. It was now two years later, and she was still alive and thriving. This same journalist came to interview her about how she made this remarkable recovery.

In the middle of the interview, she left the room to get something for both of them to drink, and he went over to a rather large organ that was in the corner of the room. On top of the organ there was this glass bowl filled with water and a condom was floating on top of it.

He thought this was kind of strange but when she came back into the room, he felt funny asking her about it and finished the interview. As he was leaving, he couldn't help but ask her about the condom floating on top of the water. She said she was taking a walk one day and saw this condom on the side of the road. The wrapper said: "For the prevention of disease keep moist and keep on your organ."

Baird Jones

A guy meets a girl in a singles bar. He says, "Hey, you wanna fuck?"

She says, "Sure, your place or mine?"

He replies, "If it's going to be a hassle, forget it."

Cory Kahaney

My mother once gave me a book called *How to Marry a Rich Man*. I'll save you the twelve bucks—ready?

Here are the three things every woman needs to know:

Chapter 1: Bald can be beautiful.

Chapter 2: Height is highly overrated.

Chapter 3: Not everyone likes anal sex but then again not everyone gets to drive a Porsche.

Kenny Kramer

It's a gated community built around a golf course. Sol decides to play a round. The starter asks him if he wouldn't mind playing with Vinny, a new member. Sol says, "Fine," and he and Vinny tee off.

At the fourth hole, Sol notices a rifle in Vinny's golf bag.

"Why are you carrying a rifle in your golf bag?" Sol wants to know.

Vinnie says, "To be honest with you, I'm a hit man for the mob."

Sol asks if he can see the gun, so Vinny takes it out and shows it to him. It's a beauty—complete with a large telescopic sight.

Vinnie claims that the sight is so dead-on powerful that he can shoot the head off a pin at a hundred yards.

Vinny says, "Every time I pull that trigger I make a thousand dollars."

Sol hands the gun back to Vinny, who happens to look through the sight. He notices a big house and he comments, "What a great looking house."

Sol says, "That's my house."

Still looking through the sight, Vinny asks, "Who's that hot blonde at the pool?"

Sol says, "That's my wife."

Vinny asks, "And who's that guy with her?"

Sol gets angry and says, "That's the pool guy—I had a feeling she was fucking around with him." Then Sol says, "Vinny, I wanna hire you right now. Put a bullet in the back of her head and then blow that bastard's cock off."

Vinny starts aiming . . . and aiming . . . and aiming. Sol's getting impatient and asks, "What are you waiting for?"

Vinny says, "Relax, I'm about to save you a thousand dollars."

Sal the Stockbroker Governale

Why do police dogs lick their balls?
To get the taste of black people out of their mouths.

Chadeo

An elephant was walking in the jungle and stepped on a sharp stick. The elephant was screaming in pain, until an ant came by and helped the elephant out. The elephant was so grateful he told the ant he would do anything to repay him. The ant thought a bit and said, "Well, I never fucked an elephant and I always wanted to."

The elephant hesitated, then said, "You did help me out, sure, it's the least I can do."

So the ant crawled up the elephant's leg, moved its tail aside, and just when the ant inserted himself a large coconut fell from a tree and hit the elephant in the head.

The elephant screamed and the ant yelled, "Yeah!!! Take it all, bitch!!!"

—

A high school student wanted to make some money, so he knocked on a neighbor's door and asked if he could shovel the driveway for $10. The neighbor said, "Sure, but do a good job."

An hour later the neighbor came out to see how it was going. The driveway was clear but on the lawn he saw the kid's name written in pee in the snow.

The neighbor was fuming and yelling at the kid, saying he wasn't going to pay and the kid had to clean it up. The kid looked at him and said, "I don't know why you're mad at me. It's your daughter's handwriting!"

—

A man was taking a shower when he realized he had no more soap left. So he got out of the shower and ran to the store. In his rush, he didn't realize he was still naked. The store owner felt bad for him, so he gave him two bars of soap for free.

On his way home, he saw some people coming his way, so he ducked into church. Then three nuns were about to spot him, so he put the bars of soap under his arms and pretended he was a statue. The nuns saw the man but didn't know what to make of him. One nun said, "I think this is one of those fancy new vending machines."

So she put a quarter in his mouth, pulled his penis, his elbow went up, and a bar of soap fell out. The nun was happy, "Look, a bar of soap." The next nun did the same, put a quarter in his mouth, pulled his penis, his elbow went up, and she got a bar of soap. The third nun put a quarter in his mouth, pulled his penis, and nothing happened. She pulled his penis again and nothing. She kept pulling and pulling and finally she was like, "Look! Ivory Liquid!"

Aubrey Reuben

I said to this girl, "Put your hand in my pocket."
She said, "I can't do that. I'll feel crazy."
I said, "Oh yeah? Go a little lower. You'll feel nuts."

Morris Levy

My girlfriend said to me, "Give me twelve inches and make it hurt." So I fucked her four times and punched her in the face.

Brad Trackman

Hooking up with a woman is like being a safecracker. Every woman has a different combination and it's up to us men to figure it out. And believe me, they're gonna change the combination. Every night. That's okay because men are brilliant. We know how to get into the safe. We crack it open. We say anything to get in there.

We say things like, "I don't care if you're skinny or fat, I like you for you." Twenty-two to the left. "We don't need to have sex, we can just cuddle." Thirty-four to the right.

There's nothing like getting into the safe. Except a new safe! That's the best safe. Sometimes that can be surprising. "Whew! That's a big safe! Looks like some other guys had the same combination."

Erik Von Broock

There was this really fat guy who wanted to lose weight, but no matter what diet he tried, nothing worked. Well one day, as he was reading the paper, he saw an ad that said: "Lose As Much Weight As You Want for Only $1 a Pound."

He gets really excited and calls the number provided and tells them he wants to lose ten pounds. They tell him that they will send a representative over to his house the next morning. The next morning the doorbell rings and he opens the door to find a really hot blonde with a sign on her chest—"if you catch me, you can fuck me"—and with that, she runs off.

Well, the fat guy starts chasing her, and ten miles later he catches her and they have sex. After she leaves, he checks his weight and sees that he lost the ten pounds. So the next day he calls and says he wants to lose twenty pounds. Same thing happens. He chases the hot blonde, this time for twenty miles, catches her, fucks her like crazy, and in the process loses twenty pounds.

Well, the next day he decides that the thirty pounds he lost so far are not enough, so he calls them up and tells them that he wants to lose fifty pounds. The person on the other line says, "Sir, are you sure? That's really too much weight to lose all at once."

The fat guy's like, "Don't worry. I know what I'm doing." So they say that they'll send a representative over to his house the next morning. The next morning he wakes up to the ringing doorbell. Excited about the prospect of losing more weight and screwing a hot chick, he jumps out of the bed, opens the door, and finds himself face to face with a *huge* gorilla. And the gorilla's wearing a sign on its chest: "If I catch you, I'll fuck the living shit out of you."

Alli Joseph

A bear and a rabbit are taking a shit in the woods together, and the bear says to the rabbit, "Hey, rabbit, I have a question for you."

Rabbit says, "What's that?"

Bear says, "Do you have a problem with shit sticking to your fur?"

Rabbit says, "No, can't say that I do."

So the bear wipes his ass with the rabbit.

Frankie Hudak

Two gay guys are home one night bored out of their minds, and one says to the other, "I'm bored."

The other says "Yeah, me too."

The first guy has a moment of inspiration and says, "Hey, I got an idea. Let's play Hide and Go Seek."

The second guy says, "Yeah . . . okay . . . let's play."

So the first guy says, "I'll hide and if you find me, I'll blow you."

The second guy says, "What if I can't find you?"

The first guy says, "Don't worry, I'll be behind the couch."

Gina Brillon

My brother's gay. I was so happy when he came out, because for the longest time I thought I was the only one who liked anal.

—

I dated a thug for a while. Our sex life was so weird; every time he finished, he dedicated it to a dead homey.

Bill Boggs

There's this husband and wife, and every time they want to have sex, without the kids knowing, they use another term for it. Like a secret language. The code is, "Honey, let's do the laundry."

One night after hosting a party, the husband says to his wife, "Honey, let's do the laundry."

And the wife says, "No, babe, I'm too tired, maybe later."

So the husband slinks off and goes to bed dejected. A couple of hours later, he asks again, and once more she turns him down. The wife wakes up toward morning, feeling bad that she turned her husband down. So she wakes him up and says, "Honey, let's do the laundry now."

And the husband goes, "Sorry, babe, it was a small load, so I did it by hand."

Doug Dechert

Three black southern women are sitting around a shack, peeling potatoes and shucking corn, and talking about their men. Their names are Lavinia, Lawanda, and Ulivia.

Ulivia says in a bragging kind of way, "My man's got a dick that's ten inches long and five inches thick."

Lawanda says, "That's nothing. My man's got a dick twelve inches long and six inches thick."

Lavinia says, "I don't have no need for no big dick, 'cause my man's a Courvoisier."

Both ladies ask, "What's a Courvoisier?"

"He's a fancy 'licker.'"

Arie Kaplan

A businessman lost all his money, so he decides to spend his last twenty bucks at a whorehouse. He goes up to the madam and asks her what he could get for $20. The madam gives him a lengthy stare and tells him to go upstairs, last door on the left. He proceeds to go up the stairs and enters the room. Inside, to his amazement, he sees a gorgeous blonde waiting naked on the bed. So he tears off his clothes, jumps on top of her, and starts pumping away for dear life. But after a few minutes into it, he looks and realizes that she's got something white gushing from her nose and eyes! He flips out and runs downstairs. He finds the madam and tells her, "There's something wrong with the girl you gave me! She's got white stuff leaking from her nose and eyes! I think she's really sick or something!"

Without blinking, the madam calmly picks up a phone and yells, "Harold, the dead one's full again."

Andy Tsagaris

My neighbor always complains his wife doesn't like sex. I find that hard to believe. Last night we did it twice.

—

I tried phone sex once, but the phone wasn't in the mood.

Tammy Faye Starlight

What does a Jewish pedophile say?
Hey kid, wanna buy some candy?

Lisa Lampanelli

Ladies, stop with those unnecessary surgeries. Stop with the tit implants, the Botox lips, and the collagen head. And stop with that cunt wax! Stop with the cunt wax! Just date a black guy—

With Lisa Lampanelli. "If you could just see where my other hand was, you'd know why she's reacting like this. Actually, I asked her to show me how wide she has to open to handle her boyfriend."

they're happy rummaging around a jungle down there. "Are you kiddin' me!?! I ain't shavin' this, mothafucka! I been on TV! This is celebrity bush! Hey, Kunte Kinte, get down there and get one caught in your grille."

—

What do you call a black woman who's had seven abortions? A crime fighter.

—

How many Spics does it take to clean a bathroom?
None. That's a nigger's job

Wendel

What's the worst thing about fucking ten-year-old boys?
Getting the blood out of the clown suits!

Jim Vern

One hooker says to another hooker, "Do you smoke while you're doing it?"
The other hooker says, "I don't know, I never looked."

—

A john picks up a hooker on the street. They go to a motel and get ready to have sex.
The hooker says, "Do you want to try something kinky?"
The john says, "Why not?"
The hooker has a glass eye, takes it out, and tells the guy to fuck her in the eye socket.
After he's done, the john says, "That was the kinkiest sex I ever had, can we do again?"
The hooker says, "Sure, I work this block all the time. I'll keep an eye out for you."

Lenny Marcus

A customer walks into a deli that has a sign on the wall that says, "You want it we have it."

The customer says to the deli guy, "You mean to try and tell me you have anything I could want?"

The deli guy says, "That's what the sign says."

So the customer asks, "Okay, give me a quarter pound of elephant cock."

The deli guy just stares at him.

The customer says, "Aha—see, you don't have it, do you?"

The deli guy looks at him and says, "We have it. But you want me to open a whole elephant cock for a lousy quarter of a pound?"

—

A guy goes to visit his friend who just went though a messy divorce. He walks into the divorcee's house and the guy is sitting quietly in a chair facing an empty wall that has wires sticking out of it.

The only thing left is a VCR on the floor with a tampon on it. The friend looks at the tampon on the VCR and says, "What's this?"

The guys looks at him and says, "It's to remind me of the cunt who took the television set."

Stacey Prussman

Some strange guy on the subway said to me, "Let's go back to my place and do a little sixty-nine."

I said to him, "How about you go back to your place and do a little ninety-six?"

He replied, "What kind of position is that?"

I said, "That's when you go home alone and can go fuck yourself."

—

I don't wanna say my boyfriend's penis is small. Let's just say when I give him a hand job, I feel like I'm thumb wrestling with him.

Kerri Louise

Why did God give women yeast infections?
So they would understand what it's like to live with an irritating cunt.

—

What's the difference between Michael Jackson and acne?
At least acne waits till you're twelve to come on your face.

—

Why do they call PMS, PMS?
Because Mad Cow Disease was already taken.

—

A little boy says to his father, "Daddy, what does a vagina look like?"
The father says, "Well son, before sex it looks like a beautiful flower about to bloom. And after sex, it looks like a pit bull eating mayonnaise."

Tom Cotter

A little boy is in the bathtub with his mother.
He points between her legs and says, "Mommy, what is that?"
The mother is caught off guard and a bit flustered. She says, "Well, honey, that's a hatchet wound."
The little boy says, "Nice shot . . . right in the cunt."

—

Why do tampons have strings?
So that crabs can bungee jump.

—

What is twelve inches long and hangs between a little boy's legs?
Michael Jackson's necktie.

—

What are the small bumps around a woman's nipples for?
It's Braille for "suck here."

—

What is an Australian kiss?
It is the same as a French kiss, but only down under.

—

What do you do with 365 used condoms?
Melt them down, make a tire, and call it a Goodyear.

—

Why are hurricanes normally named after women?
When they come they're wild and wet, but when they go, they take your house and car with them.

—

Why do girls rub their eyes when they get up in the morning?
They don't have balls to scratch.

Jim David

A farmer was depressed and said to a friend, "My crops are down, my wife left me, I'm broke. I need something."

His friend said, "Go down to the whorehouse. Take one of your ducks. Talk to Monica. She will have sex with you if you give her the duck."

The farmer went to the whorehouse and said, "I'm broke, but if you have sex with me, you can have the duck."

Monica said, "Sure."

They had sex. Monica said, "That was the most incredible sex I have ever had. In fact, let's do it again, for free."

They did it again, and Monica said, "Whew. Wow. Listen, you have to have sex with the madam. In fact, that was so much fun,

you can have the duck back. But go have sex with the madam."
The farmer saw the madam, and she was grotesque. He snuck out
with the duck under his arm. As he returned, his friend saw him
and said, "Looks like you didn't make out too well."

The farmer said, "The hell I didn't. I got a fuck for a duck, a
duck for a fuck, I ducked a fuck, and I still got the fuckin' duck."

—

Jesse James gets onto a train and says, "I'm gonna rape all the
men, and rob all the women."

This woman says, "Don't you mean rape all the women and rob
all the men?"

A gay guy in the back stands up and says, "'Scuse me, I believe
Mr. James knows how to rob a train."

—

How do you get a nun pregnant?
You fuck her.

Julie Goldman

Jesus was nailed to the cross. Bang, bang they hammered one
hand in. Bang, bang, they hammered the other hand in. Jesus peers
out in pain and exclaims, "Hey! I can see my house from here!"

—

A woman walks into a bar. She orders a Coors Light. Then two,
then three. The bartender keeps filling her up and so do the lech-
erous guys at the bar. She is totally wasted.

The bartender says, "Hey, let's rape her." So they do.

She comes in the next night. She orders the same Coors light,
and drinks them till she can't stand up.

Once again the bartender says, "Hey, let's rape her." So they do.

The next night she comes in. This time she orders a Miller light.
The bartender asks, "Hey, whatta ya changing beers tonight? Don't
like the Coors anymore?"

She says, "Yeah, but I can't drink Coors Lights anymore. They make my pussy hurt."

Jorjeana Marie

My dad would sit at the dinner table and say things like, "Eat something! You're getting too thin! Pretty soon you're gonna fall right through your asshole and hang yourself!"

Johnny Cigar

Little Johnny was given $20 by his dad to lose his virginity to a hooker. On the way there, he stopped by his grandma's house for cookies.

Grandma asked, "Where are you heading to, little Johnny?"

And Johnny replied, "Dad gave me money to go lose my virginity to a hooker."

Grandma said, "Oh, well, just give me the $20 and I'll fuck you."

When little Johnny went home, Dad asked him, "So, big John, how did it go with the hooker?"

Little Johnny replied, "I never got to her. Grandma fucked me instead."

Dad said, "You fucked my mother???!!!!!"

Little Johnny replied, "Well . . . now you know how I feel!"

Montgomery Frazier

Two blondes were walking through the woods when one looked down and said, "Oh, look at the deer tracks."

The other blonde looks and says, "Those aren't deer tracks, those are wolf tracks."

"No, those are deer tracks."

They keep arguing and arguing, and half an hour later they were both killed by a train.

—

What is the difference between a blonde and a mosquito?
The mosquito stops sucking after you smack it.

Jon Fisch

When I hang out with my gay friend, I know everyone thinks we're a couple. The other day we were hanging out and this nice looking lady was coming toward us and I didn't want her to think I was gay, so I tried to think of something non-gay to say. She came toward us. I looked at her, and I looked at my friend, and I looked back at her, and I just sort of panicked and shouted, "I love to eat pussy!"

Billy Bingo

After learning a woman won over $1 million in a lawsuit for spilling hot coffee on her lap at a McDonald's, my wife decided to try it. She pulled up to the drive-through, ordered a sixteen-ounce cup of black coffee, then put it between her legs. It *froze*!

Marie Milito

A guy wakes up, looks in the mirror, and sees a red spot in the middle of his forehead. He calls the doctor, goes to see him, and has some tests done. The doctor calls the next day and tells him to come into the office to talk. The guy is now worried and asks if he's dying. The doctor says, "No, but I'd rather we chat in person."

He gets to the office and the doctor explains that he's never seen this condition before but it does have a name and he can explain it.

The guy is growing a penis out of that spot. So the guy is now freaked out and asks how long it'll be before it's fully grown.

The doctor explains it will take about a year.

The guy says, "Y'mean I'll see a penis in the middle of my forehead in a year???!!"

The doctor responds, "Not really, because your balls will be covering your eyes."

Neil Lasher

God is trying to give the Ten Commandments away. He goes to Arabia and offers them to the Arabs. The Arabs ask God what the Ten Commandments are and he tells them that they are rules to live by. The Arabs ask for an example and God says, "Thou shalt not kill." The Arabs say, "No thanks, God, we pass.

Next, God offers the Ten Commandments to the Mexicans. Again, he is asked what are the Ten Commandments. God again says that they are rules to live by. The Mexicans ask for an example and he says, "Thou shalt not steal." The Mexicans tell God that they want nothing to do with this!

Then God goes to the Jews. He tells them he has these commandments, and they are rules to live your life by.

The Jews ask, "How much are they?"

God says, "They're free!"

The Jews say, "Okay, in that case we'll take ten."

Laura Spaeth

A woman is sobbing alone on a pier when suddenly a man comes up to her and asks why she's crying. The woman says, "I'm broke. I have no love in my life and nowhere to go. I'm going to jump off this pier."

The man responds, "Don't do that. I'll tell you what. I'm a sailor and if you come with me we'll sail around the world together. I'll feed you, give you a home on the ship, and all you have to do in return is fuck me."

She thinks for a moment and then says, "Wow, what a great deal, you're on, sailor!"

So every day, the sailor keeps his promise. They take off, she fucks him, he gives her a sandwich, they dock. This is repeated daily for a couple of days. One day another man on the ship sees the woman, naked and surrounded by sandwich wrappers.

He says, "Excuse me, miss, may I ask what the hell is going on?"

She says, "Oh, my life has been saved by this wonderful sailor. He's given me a home on this beautiful ship. Every day we sail around the world, he feeds me, and in return all I have to do is fuck him."

The man responds, "You've been fucked all right, lady. This is the Staten Island Ferry!"

Nikki Chawla

What's the deal with the names of these condoms, Trojans, Ramseys . . . what do you want to do: conquer Egypt or get laid?

Peaches Rodriguez

Two middle-aged women are golfing on the greens. They're on the ninth hole, and one says to the other, "I have got to go to the bathroom so bad, but the clubhouse is a mile away."

The other one says, "Just go over there behind the bushes. I'll keep a lookout."

At the exact same time two worms are under the ground, waking up from a winter's sleep, and one says to the other, "We haven't been outside for a really long time. What say you go up top and see what the weather's like."

So the worm makes his way to the top and at the exact same time gets a soaking from the lady going pee. He climbs back down, and the other worm asks, "So what's it like up there?"

He says, "Man, its raining so hard out there that the birds are building their nests upside down!!!"

Superman is really horny one night and he's single, out flying around Metropolis. He gets this great idea to go over to Wonder Woman's house and check her out. He peeks into her window and finds that she's totally naked and all alone on her couch!

He thinks, "I can use my superspeed to go in there and, in the blink of an eye screw her and get out, she'll never know what happened."

So boom! He does it! Next thing you know, Wonder Woman gets up and says, "What the hell was that?"

The Invisible Man says, "I don't know but my asshole is killing me!"

Tony Ray Rossi

This woman goes into the beauty parlor, and she's getting ready to go on a trip to Italy. So she sits in the chair, and the hairdresser says to her, "So where are you going on your trip?"

She says, "I'm going to Rome."

He says, "Rome? Whattaya wanna go to Rome for? It's all Italians, and it's crowded, and it's hot . . . oh my God, Rome. How you getting there?"

She says, "I'm flying Delta."

He says, "Delta? Oh my God, they're never on time, the seats are so small, the food is terrible. What are you flying Delta for?"

She says, "I don't know."

He says, "So where are you staying when you get to Rome?"

She says, "I'm staying in a beautiful hotel called the Excelsior."

He says, "Oh my God, that hotel is so dingy, the beds are small, it's so run down, the food is terrible. What are you staying there for?"

She says, "I don't know."

He says, "Well what are you gonna do when you get to Rome?"

She says, "I'm gonna try to go see the Pope."

He screams, "See the Pope? You're never gonna see the Pope. You and a million other people. He's gonna look like a little piece of rice."

So he does her hair, and she leaves that day, kind of upset. She goes on her trip and comes back in to the shop a month later.

He says to her, "So how was your trip?"

"Oh my God," she says, "you won't believe it. We get to the airport, they overbooked the flight, they bumped us up to first class, no extra charge. The plane was on time, the food was great, champagne, everything on the house, we had a great flight."

He says, "Oh really. So how was the hotel?"

She says, "The hotel? The hotel was amazing. We get there. They just finished a $50 million restoration. They, too, were overbooked. They bumped us up into the presidential suite. We get in there, there's wine and cheese, and caviar, no extra charge. It was wonderful."

He says, "Oh really. Did you get to see the Pope?"

She says, "This you won't believe. We're in line, all of a sudden the Swiss Guard taps me on the shoulder. When I turn around he says, 'The Pope would like to have a private audience with a few of his followers. Would you like to come with me?'"

"So I said, 'Of course.'

"So he takes us into the back room of the Vatican, we're all standing there. All of a sudden the door opens and in walks the Pope."

The hairdresser says, "Yeah, so what did the Pope have to say?"

She says, "The Pope said, 'Who gave you that fucked-up haircut?'"

———

An Italian couple gets married, and they're gonna move in with her mother. So they go back to the house that night, and they're going to consummate the marriage. They go up to the bedroom, he takes off his pants. And he has really hairy legs.

The bride runs downstairs and says to her mother, "Ma, he's gotta really hairy a legs."

The mother says, "Lucia, you go uppa stairs. That's a your husband."

So she goes back upstairs, and this time he takes off his shirt, he has this hairy, hairy chest. She runs back downstairs, and says, "Ma, he's a gotta a hairy, hairy chest."

The mother says, "Lucia, you go back uppa stairs. That's a your husband."

She goes back upstairs, and now he's taking off his socks, and he's got a half a foot. She runs back downstairs and screams, "Ma, he's a gotta foot and a half."

The mother says, "Lucia, you stay here. I go uppa stairs."

—

This girl is deaf, and she speaks like people do who are deaf. She's really hard to understand. So her mother sends her to the fish store for five pounds of mackerel. She gets down to the fish store, and the guy says, "Can I help you?"

She says, "Fmmm pmmm mmmmm."

The guy says, "Excuse me?"

And once again she says, "Fmmm pmmm mmmmml."

He's like, "What did you say?"

She repeats it again.

He says, "Try and say it a little clearer."

With that, out of frustration, she shoves her hand down her pants, rubs it around her crotch, and puts it up to his nose.

He takes one breath and yells out, "Holy mackerel."

She goes, "Five pounds."

Karith Foster

What did one lesbian frog say to the other lesbian frog?
They're right!! We do taste like chicken!!!

—

So this cowboy gets captured by Indians, and they're going to scalp and kill him, but they're going to spare his life for three days and grant him one special request per day. On the first day, he tells the chief he needs to speak to his horse. The Indian chief thinks this is odd, but grants him his request. So the cowboy whispers something in his horse's ear—the horse takes off and is gone for a few hours.

When he returns, the horse has a beautiful blonde on his back. They go into the cowboy's tent and the Indians just roll their eyes. The second day the chief tells the cowboy he has only two requests left and he ought to use them wisely. But once again the cowboy asks to speak to his horse and whispers something in the horse's ear. The horse takes off and returns several hours later with a beautiful redhead on his back.

They go into the cowboy's tent and the Indians just roll their eyes. The chief says, "Stupid white man can only think of one thing!" So the third and last day arrives, and again the chief reminds him he only has one request left. *Again* it's to speak to his horse.

The chief grants his last request and just smiles, knowing what the cowboy asked for. So the cowboy whispers into the horse's ear.

The horse takes off, but this time he's gone all day. The moon is out and the sun's going down when finally the horse appears on the horizon. When he gets closer, all the Indians and the cowboy see that he's got a gorgeous brunette on his back. The cowboy calls the horse over, grabs him by his ears, and screams, "I said posse you fucking moron!!! P-O-S-S-E!!! Not pussy!!!"

Dr. Laurie Betito

A young man goes into a drug store to buy condoms. The pharmacist says the condoms come in packs of three, nine, or twelve and asks which the young man wants. "Well," he said, "I've been seeing this girl for a while and she's really hot. I want the condoms because I think tonight's *the* night. We're having dinner with her parents, and then we're going out and I've got a feeling I'm gonna get lucky after that. Once she's had me, she'll want me all the time, so you'd better give me the twelve-pack."

The young man makes his purchase and leaves. Later that evening, he sits down to dinner with his girlfriend and her parents.

He asks if he might say grace, and they agree. He begins the prayer, but continues praying for fifteen minutes.

The girl leans over and says, "You never told me that you were such a religious person."

He leans over to her and says, "You never told me that your father is a pharmacist!"

Sid Bernstein

A snail gets sexually assaulted by two turtles. The snail's on the witness stand. The judge says, "All right, which one of them went first?"

The snail says, "I don't know, your honor. Everything happened so fast."

Stewie Stone

So this guy comes home drunk out of his mind, the house is pitch dark, he staggers up the stairs, crawls into the bedroom, finds his wife asleep, and makes love to her in the dark in a drunken stupor.

He gets up, walks into the bathroom, and sees his wife sitting there.

She says, "Shhh, don't make any noise. Mother slept over."

Silver Saundors-Friedman

A journalist is interviewing an Orthodox rabbi, and he wants to find out what the rabbi does to help the ecology. So he asks him, "Rabbi, what do you do when you're through with the remnants of the cloths from the old clothes you collect?"

And the rabbi says, "We send it away and it comes back as a patchwork quilt."

The journalist says, "And rabbi, what do you do with the leftovers of food that you collect on the holidays?"

And the Rabbi says, "We collect it all, make it into a stew, and feed it to the homeless."

And the journalist says, "And rabbi, I always wanted to ask you. What do you do with the foreskins from circumcisions?"

The rabbi says, "Well, I'll tell you the truth. We keep them all, and we collect huge amounts of them. Then we send them away, and they come back in the form of a putz like you!"

Vinny Vella
[Vinny told me this joke in the form of a skit—with audience participation.—JLG]

VINNY: Let's say you went on a camping trip with four guys you didn't know very well, and you woke up in the morning and found a condom hanging out of your ass—would you tell anyone?

ME: No.

VINNY: Wanna go camping?

Mickey Freeman

This couple from Columbus, Ohio, is celebrating their twenty-fifth anniversary, so their family sends them to Paris, and they go to the Folies Bergere. In the middle of the show, a man comes out, puts down three walnuts on a table, unzips his pants, takes out his wang, and one, two, three, cracks all the walnuts. The couple goes backstage and tells the guy how fantastic he is. They can't get over it.

Twenty-five years later, this same couple goes back to France to celebrate their fiftieth anniversary. They go back to the Folies Bergere, and sure enough in the middle of the show, the exact same guy comes out, but this time he puts down three honeydew melons, unzips his pants, takes out his wang, and one, two, three, splits them all, right down the center. The couple can't get over it.

It's unbelievable.

They go backstage to see the guy, and they say to him, "Twenty-five years ago we came to this show, you took three walnuts and split them in half. Now, twenty-five years later, you split three honeydews. What happened?"

The guy says, "My eyes went bad."

—

Mr. Silverman is walking around the old age home where he lives telling everyone he sees, "My penis just died."

The next day, he's walking around with his fly open.

One of the attendants asked him why.

He said, "Remember yesterday I told you my penis just died? Well, today is the viewing."

Howard Feller

Mickey Mouse walks into a marriage counselor's office, and the marriage counselor says to Mickey, "Listen, you can't divorce your wife just because she's crazy."

And Mickey says, "I didn't say she was crazy, I said she was fucking Goofy."

—

An old woman comes out of the shower, opens up her bathrobe like a flasher, and says to her husband, "Superpussy."

He looks at her as if he's thinking it over and says, "I'll have the soup."

Marvin Scott

A guy goes into a tattoo shop and asks to have a $100 bill tattooed on his penis. The tattoo artist inquires, "Why do you want a $100 bill permanently on your penis?"

"Three reasons," the man answers. "One, I like to play with my money. Second, I like to watch my money grow. And third, this way my wife can blow a hundred bucks without leaving the house."

—

A tourist in a restaurant in Spain sees the waiter serving turins of soup with giant round things in the bowl, like matzo balls.

He asks the waiter what it is and he's informed "that's bull soup . . . a specialty of the house." The waiter goes on to explain that after each bullfight they serve the balls of the defeated bull. The patron is told that an order for the soup has to be placed days in advance.

The patron is so curious, he places his order, makes a reservation, and returns the following week. Finally, the turin of soup arrives and much to the patron's chagrin the balls in the soup are very small. "How come?" he asks.

The waiter responds, "You see, sir, the bull wins."

Colin Quinn
Worst Pickup Line He Ever Heard

If good looks were like concentration camps, you'd be Auschwitz.

Greg Giraldo

Such strange shit goes on in the New York subways. The other day I saw a guy peeing on a guy who was masturbating.

Danny Lobell

A Scottish couple are walking down the beach, and the woman turns to the man and says, "I bet you'll be wantin' to hold my hand."

And the guy says, "Aye, how'd you know that?"

She says, "Aach, I can see it in your eyes, luv."

And they continue walking and holding hands, and about a mile later she turns to him and says, "I bet you'll be wanting to kiss me."

And the man says, "Aye, but how did you know that?"

And she says, "Aach, I can see it in your eyes, luv."

So they kiss, and they keep walking and about a half-mile later she turns to him and says, "Aach, I bet you want to get this over with and fuck me already."

And he says, "Aye, but I bet you can't see that in me eyes."

She says, "Aach, you're right. I can tell by the tilt in your kilt."

John Morrison
Paraphrasing a Joke He Heard from Louie C. K.

Guys know that the worst thing about the World Trade Center was that they could tell what kind of an asshole they were, by how soon after the tragedy they started masturbating again. With me, I think it was between the time the first tower fell and the second.

Dean Edwards

There's these three kids all trying to prove whose father could eat the most, and the first kid says, "Well, my dad, he can eat ten Whoppers, five Big Macs, twenty supersized fries, and a gallon of cherry coke."

The second kid says, "That ain't nothin'. My dad, he can eat forty Big Macs, thirty Whoppers, twenty-nine large fries, and a river of coke."

The third kid says, "That ain't nothin'. My daddy, he can eat lightbulbs."

The first two kids look at him and say, "Whattaya mean he can eat lightbulbs?"

He says, "Last night I heard him say to my momma, hurry up and cut that light off so I can eat that thing."

Professor Irwin Corey

Ronald Reagan says to his wife, "Nancy, Nancy, as long as I have a face, you have a place to sit." She's been sitting on his face for thirty years. You can't tell where her ass ends and his face begins.

Dena Blizzard

This mom has three boys, and they're not very wealthy. It's Thanksgiving, and they have to go out and shoot their own turkey. So she gets a BB gun, shoots the turkey, and makes it for dinner.

She tells the boys, "I tried to get all the BBs out, but I'm not sure I did, so just be careful." So the boys eat the dinner, and after dinner she's cleaning up and the first boy comes running in. Crying hysterically, he says, "Mom, Mom, I was just in the bathroom peeing, and I peed a BB."

His mom says, "Oh honey, don't worry. It's okay. It's just natural. If you ate one, it'll pass."

She keeps cleaning up when the second boy runs in screaming and crying. "Mom, Mom."

She's like, "What happened?"

He says, "I was in the bathroom and I had to pee, and I peed a BB."

And she says, "Oh honey, don't worry, it's natural, it'll pass. It's not a big deal."

The third one comes in hysterical crying. "Mommy, mommy."

She says, "I know honey. You were in the bathroom and you peed a BB, right?"

He says, "No. I was jerking off and I accidentally shot the dog."

Rick Younger

So there's these two Greek fishermen, and they're out on a boat fishing, 'cause that's what Greek fishermen do, and they're out all day on the boat, and they can't catch a fish for nothing. The day is going by, and eventually the sun is about to set, and finally they both get their hooks into the same fish.

They get the fish in the boat, but they realize the fish is too small to share, so they have to figure out who gets to keep the fish. So one fisherman says to the other, "Whoever's the manliest of the two of us gets to keep the fish."

The other guy says, "How do we decide who's the manliest?"

The first guy says, "Well, we gotta have sex with each other, and the one who can take it the longest gets to keep the fish."

The second guy says, "Okay that seems fair. I'll go first."

So he starts giving the other guy the pounding of his life, like pow, pow, pow. It seems like it's going on for hours. Finally, he finishes and the guy he was doing says, "Okay, my turn."

And the other guy says, "That's okay. You keep the fish."

Marion Grodin

I am recently single and my friends tell me I should go on the Internet, you know 'cause everybody's going on the Internet looking for love. But whenever I go on the Internet, it seems to me there are basically two categories of men out there: guys looking for bigger genitals and lower mortgages. So according to the Internet, you'd think the whole planet was just filled with little-dicked guys waiting to refinance.

Gene Cornish

So there's a family gathering, and there's a lot of people . . . mothers, fathers, kids, and this guy wants to tell a joke, but it's kind of dirty. So what he does is he says to everybody, this joke has a couple of foul words in it, so when it gets to a foul word, I'll raise my hand as a warning so that if you want to you can leave, and I won't offend anybody. So remember, I'll tell the joke, but when I raise my hand, be ready for the foul words. So here's how the joke goes, "These two cocksuckers walk into a bar . . ."

Tony Woods

So I used to have a girlfriend. And it was purely sex. That's all it was. But it wasn't just sex, it was the best fuckin' pussy I ever had in my life. I mean, it would give me convulsions, this is how sex was with this woman.

It would send me into screaming fits, and sometimes I would leave her apartment in the middle of the night, because you know, I was still married of course, and I'd walk out into the hallway and her neighbors would stick their head out of their door, and say, "Ohh, I'm glad you're leaving."

And this one guy goes "Whoa, you are the man! I could hear her screaming way down the hall."

And I'm like, "That wasn't her. That was me."

So this goes on for a while. I go back two weeks later and me and this girl are having sex again. It's always regular. It's like ESPN sex. We could watch the game and still do it. But then after maybe two or three minutes of boom, boom, boom, boom, boom, this feeling kicks in, and I start screaming, "Aaah, aaaah, aaaah," and digging my nails into her back, and I start screaming, and working, working, working, and I yell out, "This is the best pussy I ever had in my fuckin' life."

And she said to me, "Yeah, that's it. Talk to me."

I'm like, "Bitch, that was all I was gonna say." So I thought about what was on my mind, and I said, "I gotta fart."

So she was into it, and she said, "Do what you gotta do."

So I let loose with a long one, and right then the cat screams out, and scratches my ass, and at that moment I realized, the pussy wasn't that good. The cat had been behind me the whole time, licking my balls.

And right then I told her, "This is fuckin' nasty. I'm going back to my wife. Don't call me, and I won't call you. C'mon, kitty. Let's get the fuck out of here."

Buck Wolf

My niece is seventeen years old. She's kind of a tomboy. She always wears pants and all, and one day the subject of lesbianism came up, and she just doesn't want to talk about sex.

So I said, "Hey, Michelle, what do you call a lesbian dinosaur?"

She's like, "I give up . . . what?"

I said, "A Lick-a-Lotopuss."

Samantha Cole

A couple just got married, and on their honeymoon night she confesses to him that she's still a virgin.

He's like, "How is that possible? You've been married three times already."

She's like, "Well, the first husband was a gynecologist, and all he wanted to do was open it up and look at it. The second one was a psychiatrist, and all he wanted to do was ask me how I felt about it. And the third husband was a stamp collector, and all he wanted to do was . . . boy do I miss him!!!"

Sir Ivan Wilzig

Two guys are sitting at the bar. One happens to mention to the other that he's about to get married to the waitress from the restaurant up the block.

The other guy says, "Alice? I've known that tramp for ten years. Blond hair with a mole on her inner thigh?"

"Yeah, that's her," says the fiancé.

"She has a tattoo on her lower back of a penis pointing to her asshole?" the guy says.

The fiancé says, "Yeah, that's right."

"She's into all kinds of kinky shit, and gets off on blowing two guys at the same time, right?"

"That's her," says the fiancé.

"I must have fucked that skank a thousand times."

With that, the fiancé calls over the bartender and says, "Next drink's on me. This guy's a friend of my fiancée."

Aesha Waks

This fifty-year-old man leaves a disturbing note for his wife.

She comes home to read the note lying on their bed saying, "You know I love you but I'm going through a midlife crisis. I'm with my eighteen-year-old secretary in a hotel. Be home at 11."

Well, his wife was outraged, but had a little plan of her own, so she writes back, "I, too, am going through a midlife crisis, so I'm going to a hotel with my eighteen-year-old tennis instructor, but I'll be home in three days because eighteen goes into fifty way more than fifty could ever go into eighteen!"

King

One night I was working the rope at Spy, when this girl comes up to me with this other girl behind her and says, "I will give you the best blow job of your life guaranteed with my sister if you let us in."

So I take them into this back hallway we have and let them go to work. One's licking me, one's blowing me, one's doing this, and one's doing that, and it was really good, but it wasn't the best. And they'd guaranteed it would be the best, so I took them both back outside and wouldn't let them in.

Then some other guy comes up, and he wants to come in, and he was just ridiculous looking. I told him, "I got good news and bad news for you. Which one do you want first?"

The guy's like, "Let me get the bad news."

I'm like, "Okay, you're ugly, your breath stinks, you're dressed funny, and there's no way in hell I'm ever letting you into any club I ever work in."

He's like, "Oh, well what's the good news?" I'm like, "You see those two sisters over there? They just blew me."

Paul Provenza

[Paul did something very unusual for this book. He not only gave us jokes but also analyzed why he thought they were funny or interesting above and beyond just funny. He's either a very smart man or incredibly sick. We'll let him tell you what he told us, after we asked him to do the Aristocrats joke.—JLG & TW]

I'll just give you a handful of my favorites and tell you why these jokes are interesting to me. I don't think I'm going to do the Aristocrats *joke*, because I don't actually have a *hard and*

With Paul Provenza, an expert in the art of Jewish self-defense. Here he is applying the deadly "face-squeeze."

fast version *of it*—It's one of those things that changes all the time, *and I can't really commit to one version to be out there for posterity.*

Committing to a version of that joke just completely undermines the freedom and liberty of the joke, *and the beauty of it gets lost in the process.* So whenever anybody asks me for my version, I say, "The movie was my version," 'cause that's really the truth. *The movie is all about the subculture of it, the spontaneity of it, the freedom and amorphousness of it, and that's what makes the joke so fun and interesting in the first place.*

Plus, whenever I tell the Aristocrats, people expect it to be like the best fuckin' version ever . . . and that just isn't possible. I can't handle that kind of pressure. Fuck you. Isn't it enough you got a goddam book deal just to type shit everyone else is writing for you, you filthy hooknosed, thieving Jew? [The only comics I ever met more Jewish than Provenza were Dick Capri and Frank Chindamo.—JLG]

———

Pretty funny coming from a guy who did that with a whole damn movie, dontcha think?

All I *can tell you* is that, were I to sit down and really work at writing the best version I could possibly work out, I know there are a few elements it would contain.

Number one: It takes place in Abu Ghraib,—*probably in front of a huge backdrop of a cartoon of Saddam Hussein being blown by Osama bin Laden.*

———

Number two: Somehow they wheel in Terry Schiavo. *There'd be some jizzing down feeding tubes I'm guessing. The audience loves it 'cause she's so vulnerable.*

Number three: It *would* incorporate the *poetic imagery of the* phrase "arcing ropes of cum." *I feel that phrase lends a certain literary quality to the whole thing, and it's a phrase one rarely gets to use much.*

—

So those are a few elements I know would be in it if I were forced to commit today. Beyond that, write your own fuckin' joke. So instead of the Aristocrats, here's a few other jokes I'm particularly thrilled to know. The reason I love this joke I'm about to tell you, which is one of my all-time favorite jokes, is because it separates the men from the boys, as it *were*—This is one of those "barometer" jokes. People either get it, and they love it, or they don't get it at all, and then you know you need to stop wasting time hanging out with *those* people.

—

A little kid, about seven or eight years old, coming home from school, passes by a construction site. Goes up to the top. He's playing with his friends. They're playing King of the Hill and *Superman.* He stands up on the top of this mountain of rubble, and in the midst of the rubble he sees this rusty old welder's mask. He can't believe it. He reaches down and puts it on his head. It's the coolest thing. He flips it up and down, and he's standing up there, and he's yelling, "I'm Iron Man, I'm Iron Man."

All the other kids are jealous. Anyway, the sun's going down, it's time to go home. He starts walking home with his welder's mask on his head. Suddenly, a big stretch limo pulls up next to him, the window comes down, this old guy in the backseat says to him, "Hey kid, you ever ride in a stretch limo before?"

Kid says, "Uh, uh."

The old guy says, "Hop in."

The kid hops in, and he's so excited. He thinks to himself, "I can't believe this. First, I find this cool welder's helmet. Now I'm riding in a stretch limo. This is unbelievable."

The old guy leans over to him and says, "Hey kid. Do you know what fellatio is?"

The kid says, "Uh, uh."

They drive a little more. The guy goes, "Kid, do you know what sodomy is?"

The kid says, "Uh, uh." They drive a little more.

The guy goes, "Kid, you know what analingus is."

The kid says, "Uh, uh. But mister, maybe I better tell you. I'm not really a welder."

—

So this guy walks into a bar and he's got a big round orange head. He sits down at the bar and orders a Scotch.

The bartender leans over and says, "I don't wanna be rude, but I never saw anything like that before. What happened to your head?"

The guy goes, "Interesting story. I learned a lot about life. I was walking down a beach and found a magic lantern. I pick it up, I rub it, a genie comes out, and the genie says to me I have three wishes.

"So I wish for vast sums of money . . . huge wealth, and poof, that's how I own the empire I own today. Then I asked for a beautiful woman, a soul mate, someone who understands me, and will always be by my side. And who can give me the best sex I ever had. And that's how I met my beautiful perfect wife.

"The genie said I have one more wish, and here's where I think I went horribly, horribly wrong. I said, "Why don't you give me a big, round orange head?"

—

Two Siamese twins are at home practicing the trombone, bah-bah-bah-bah-bah, bah-bah-bah-bah-bah, and one's looking through the paper and starts yelling, "Oh my God, oh my God, Julio Iglesias is performing in town, Julio Iglesias is coming to town, we'll get to see Julio Iglesias live."

They call for tickets, they show up for the show. They get front-row seats, they're in there, they got their trombone with them. The show is over. They had the most amazing time. They go backstage and say, "We really want to meet Julio Iglesias, we really want to meet Julio Iglesias."

So they're waiting, and he finally comes out, they're standing there in their sexy outfits, playing the trombone, bah-bah-bah-bah-bah, bah-bah-bah-bah-bah, and he's like, "Hi girls, why don't you come on in."

So they come in, and they schmooze him, and they are on cloud nine. They can't believe it. It's the most amazing day. And eventually they end up fucking him. And they're fucking him, one of them's sucking him, the other one's playing bah-bah-bah-bah-bah, the other one's getting fucked up the ass while the other one's bah-bah-bah-bah-bah.

This goes on for hours. They finish, they go home. It's the most amazing thing. They can't believe it.

Two years later, they're home practicing the trombone. One of them's leafing through the paper, and starts screaming, "Julio Iglesias is coming back to town, Julio Iglesias is coming back to town. We'll have to go and see him, we'll have to go and meet him again."

The other one goes, "Do you think he'll remember us?"

—

George Carlin calls me up one day, I answer the phone and all I hear is, "Why don't men sleep with women in the morning?"

I said, "Why?"

He said, "Did you ever try and open a grilled cheese sandwich?"

[*Click. Even over the phone, a pro knows how to close strong.*]

Jim Norton

What's the best part about fucking twenty eight-year-olds? There's twenty of them.

P. J. Landers

A guy says to his wife, "I'm in the mood for some kinky sex. Can I come in your ear?"

And she says, "No, I'm afraid I'll go deaf."

He says, "Why would you say that? I've been coming in your mouth for twenty years, and you haven't stopped talking for a minute."

Rick Shapiro

I hate these reality shows where they take a woman and they designate her as ugly, like, "Your family and friends think you're hideous, and we're gonna make you better looking. You're finally gonna be acceptable, all right?" And the family's all excited, the husband's like, "We're changin' her. We're changin' her. You gotta come see her. We're guttin' my wife's vagina. We're rippin' the whole thing down, and puttin' up a new one. She's gonna be gorgeous.

"We're puttin' in a rollaway couch, a pinball machine, a full menu, a VIP room. It's a mess now. My wife won't even let me go down and look at it. Nothin' but nails and some spacklin'. Sometimes I go down there to do some thinkin', some dreamin', some quiet time.

"I'm also rippin' my nuts out, and puttin' in a Glock Desert Storm commemorative pistol, a couple of real smoke wagons (that's Texas talk for six-guns). Also we're coming around the back of my wife, putting a new sphincter in, the kind the kids can play with. When it's done it's gonna be a fun time till midnight, so come down to my wife's vagina. Even if you ain't got time, just stick your fuckin' head in."

Jason Alexander

This married woman is bored with her sex life, so she goes to a sex therapist and he says to her, "Why don't you try sixty-nine?"

Coauthor Jeffrey Gurian with Jason Alexander. "Jason's look of disbelief was a reaction to me confiding in him that I was as well-endowed as Milton Berle."

She says, "I don't know what that is."

So he explains it to her. She's very excited. She goes home, her husband comes home, and she tells him she went to a sex therapist today, and he taught her something new and fabulous called sixty-nine.

The husband says, "What is that?"

She says, "We'll just do our thing and I'll show you when we get there."

So they go into the bedroom, and they're having sex, and they're doing their thing, she sidles down into position, and just as they get into position, she farts right in his face. And she's mortified, absolutely mortified.

He's like, "It's okay, honey. Don't worry about it."

So she finally composes herself, and they kind of get back into it, and the moment is right, and she gets herself into position, and once again she farts in his face.

She's so upset, she's beside herself. She runs into the bathroom, splashes water on her face, comes back out, and he's nowhere to be found. Finally, she finds him, and he's hiding under the bed.

She says, "Honey, what are you doing under the bed?"

He says, "Sweetheart, I love you, but if you think we're doing this sixty-seven more times, you're out of your fucking mind."

Evan Steinberg

Pick-up line: If you were a necrophiliac, I swear I'd kill myself.

Roz

I encourage ladies to continue to suck dick. They don't know that you gotta do that for health reasons. Ladies, I just did some research on the power of a blow job. Do you know that one drop of sperm has the same amount of protein as sixteen Nutra-Grain bars? You mean I've been eatin' all these Nutra-Grain bars, and all I needed was one dick in my mouth? I say, "Fuck milk. Dick does a body good!!!"

Joe DeVito

I don't talk when I'm having sex, because I know I'm not gonna say anything sexy, and I'm not gonna make any sexy faces either. And that's why I always wear a ski mask when I make love.

———

A guy goes to a whorehouse in Vegas. All he wants to do is eat pussy, so he's sent upstairs to the third door on the left. Inside is a beautiful redhead. She uncrosses her legs and says to him, "Okay, big boy. You like to eat pussy? Well, chow down."

The guy hops on the bed and starts licking the whore's snatch. Something gets stuck to his tongue. It's a little piece of a carrot. He spits it out and goes on licking, then he gets a green pea stuck to his tongue. He spits it out and continues to eat her snatch. A little piece of potato ends up in his mouth.

He spits it out and asks the whore, "Are you sick or something?"

The whore says, "No, but the guy before you was."

Jimmy Carr

I fantasize about having sex with a gymnast. Not just because they're really bendy and flexible but also because I imagine they do a brilliant dismount. They end up by the side of the bed with their legs straight, and if they bend their knees just a little bit, you can make them do it again.

Drew Carey

A guy goes into a bank and says, "I wanna open up a fuckin' checking account."

And the woman says, "Sir, you have to watch your language."

And the guy says, "Fuck the language. I wanna open up a motherfucking checking account."

She goes, "That's it. I'm getting the manager."

She gets the manager, the manager goes, "What's the matter here?"

The guy goes, "I just won $20 million in the lottery, and I wanna open up a fucking checking account."

And the manager says, "And is this cunt giving you trouble?"

Todd Lynn

What's the definition of *making love*?

That's what a woman is doing while a guy is fucking her!

Chris Mata

Remember that whole "soldiers raping Iraqi citizens" debacle?

Five U.S. soldiers were charged in the Iraq rape. Two others paid cash!

Joe Starr

What do you get when you put eight fetuses into a blender and hit pulse?

I don't know. I was too busy jerkin' off!

—

A six-year-old boy gets a puppy for his birthday. His parents take him to the North Shore of Long Island, up on the cliffs. The puppy's running around, the kid's running around. They're having a great day. All of a sudden a seagull takes off on the edge of the cliff. The puppy doesn't know any better, and dives after the sea-gull right off the edge of the cliff.

The father reaches out and catches the puppy right before he goes over, but the father's losing his balance. The mother wraps herself around the father's ankles. The mother, the father, the puppy go tumbling hundreds of feet.

They're dead on the rocks, with the six-year-old boy still stand-ing up on top of the cliffs crying.

A man comes by and goes, "What happened?"

The little boy tells him, "Today's my sixth birthday. My parents got me a puppy. They fell down the cliff. They're laying down there dead."

The man says, "Oh my God."

The man unzips his fly, whips out his cock, and goes, "Today just ain't your day, kid."

Vic Henley

An Israeli girl wants to marry an Arab guy, and her family's very upset when she announces it's gonna happen, but she says to them, "Look, he's an oil-rich millionaire. We will never want for anything. Everything will be perfect. He's good to me. We'll have a wonderful life."

The family goes, "Well, we're reluctant, but okay. Whatever you want."

Ten years go by. They're celebrating their ten-year anniversary. They got kids. It's a big happy family, a perfect multicultural experience.

Her mom comes back to her and says, "You know, I gotta tell you, early on we really had a lot of misgivings, but ten years, he's been a great husband. Everything you said came true."

The girl says, "Well, you know, actually, I didn't know he was addicted to anal sex like he was. Had I known that . . . I'm actually thinking about getting a divorce. I don't know if this is working out. When we started our marriage, my asshole was the size of a dime. And now it's about as big around as a silver dollar."

And her mother says, "Are you telling me you're gonna let ninety cents come between you and all this happiness?"

———

There's a biker sittin' on the back steps of a diner, out back by the dumpster eatin' a big bowl of chili. A homeless guy's wandering through the alley, pickin' up different garbage can lids and lookin' at stuff.

The biker's like, "Hey man, c'mon, have some chili. I've missed a few meals myself. I know what it's like."

The homeless guy digs into the bowl of chili, starts scarfing it down like there's no tomorrow, gets almost to the bottom, sees a turd in the bottom of the bowl, and vomits, aaaaaaaaaaaaaaaaaaa-aaargh, all of what he ate back into the bowl, and the biker looks at him and goes, "Yeah, that's as far as I got, too!"

Chuck Nice

A guy's in a bar and he's so drunk he throws up all over his shirt. He's afraid to go home like that 'cause he knows his wife will kill him. Another guy says, "Here's what you do. This'll be great. Put $20 in your pocket, and tell your wife some guy accidentally threw up on you and he gave you this money to help pay for the cleaning."

The guy says, "Great idea."

He goes home, tells his wife the story, hands her the money, and she says, "Okay, but how come there's $40 here?"

The guy says, "He accidentally shit in my pants, too!"

Mike Birbiglia

Some people are very confident about sex. They even videotape themselves, which I never understood. After I have sex, all I can think is, "At least no one saw that."

I never once thought, "I wish I got that one in the books."

That's why I get so uncomfortable when I watch the show *Real Sex* on HBO. It's always these unwieldy middle-aged couples masturbating in a circle, on a mountain somewhere, and I know in five years from now they're gonna come to their senses and be like, "I wasn't masturbating on television, was I? Oh, noooooooo! I didn't high-five cocks with the instructor, did I? Oh, dear God."

Jim McCue

They say that beauty is only skin deep.
For me it's about nine inches.

Steve Rossi

President Bush and Dick Cheney go into a restaurant. The waitress comes over and says, "Mr. President, do you know what you want?"

President Bush says, "Yes. I'll have a quickie."

The waitress leaves all flustered and nervous.

Cheney turns to the president and says, "Mr. President, it's pronounced 'Quiche!'"

Eha Urbsalu

One afternoon a little girl excitedly approached her mother, and announced that she had learned where babies come from at school that day. Amused, her mother replied, "Really, sweetie? Why don't you tell me all about it?"

The little girl explained, "Well . . . okay . . . The mommy and daddy take off all of their clothes, and the daddy's thing sort of stands up, and the mommy puts it in her mouth, and then it sort of explodes, and that's where babies come from."

Her mom shook her head, leaned over to meet her eye to eye, and said, "Oh, honey, that's sweet, but that's not where babies come from. That's where jewelry comes from."

Bryan Kennedy

When Jane first met Tarzan of the Jungle, she was attracted to him, and during her questions about his life, she asked him how he had sex. "Tarzan not know sex," he replied. Jane explained to him what sex was.

Tarzan said, "Oh, Tarzan use hole in trunk of tree."

Horrified, she said, "Tarzan, you have it all wrong, but I will show you how to do it properly."

She took off her clothes and lay down on the ground.

"Here," she said. "You must put it in here." Tarzan removed his loincloth, stepped closer with his huge erection, and then gave her a tremendous kick right in the pussy. Jane rolled around in agony for what seemed like an eternity. Eventually, she managed to gasp for air and screamed, "What the fuck did you do that for?"

"Tarzan check for bees."

Jeffrey Gurian

About Hugh Hefner

Hefner tries to take care of his body, but at seventy-five what can you expect? At this point, he's hanging so low, he carries his sack in a wheelbarrow.

As a matter of fact, he almost didn't make it here today. On his way in this afternoon, he tripped and accidentally kicked himself in the balls.

—

About Al Sharpton

Al Sharpton's lost a lot of weight this past year. He had to. It was interfering with his sex life. He could hardly get his cock to his mouth.

Now that he's thin, Al has a very active sex life. Five or six times a day, he puts on romantic music and shoves his thumb up his ass.

—

About Gilbert Gottfried

If it wasn't for his family, he wouldn't have any sex at all.

—

About Lisa Lampanelli

Then there's Lisa Lampanelli, who recently took a part time job as the night depository slot at an all night sperm bank.

—

About Ice-T

Ice-T really likes to try and keep in shape. Three times a week he goes to the gym and lifts whites.

—

About Rob Reiner

Rob Reiner is boring as shit! Rob is so boring, he once fucked a girl and her cunt fell asleep.

Biographies

Jason Alexander is a veteran television, film and musical theater actor best known for his role as George Costanza on the hit TV series *Seinfeld*.

Ted Alexandro (www.tedalexandro.com) is one of the fastest rising young comedians in the country. He has appeared on *The Late Show with David Letterman*, *Late Night with Conan O'Brien*, *Jimmy Kimmel Live*, *The View*, and two half-hour specials on Comedy Central.

Leo Allen (www.slovinandallen.com) is one-half of the comedy team Slovin & Allen. He has worked as a staff writer on *Saturday Night Live and has appeared on Comedy Central and Late Night with Conan O'Brien*.

Julius Alvin is the author of a dozen jokebooks and the pseudonym of someone you've probably never heard of anyway.

Joe Amiel is formerly the chairman of Manhattan Pictures International.

Larry Amoros is a playwright and writer-producer for television and concert series whose current projects include *Simply Sketch* for the Logo Network and the 2006 ESPY Awards for ESPN. He also serves as a head writer for the Friars Club Roasts and is a consulting producer for the PBS news magazine *California Connected*. He is currently developing the comedy series *An Affair to Remember* for SONY TV.

Amy Anderson (www.amyanderson.net) is a nationally touring stand-up comic based in Los Angeles. Her television credits include Comedy Central's *Premium Blend*, VH1, and MTV. She is also the founder and creator of Chop-Shtick Comedy.

Ann Anello (www.consultfirst.com) is an internationally recognized singer and songwriter who has appeared all over the world and performed with everyone from Frank Sinatra, Sammy Davis Jr., and Bob Hope to Carly Simon, Cary Grant, Brett Butler and Jackie Mason. Her original music can be heard on *Guiding Light* and *One Life to Live,* and she wrote and performed "America" for the Statue of Liberty Centennial Celebration, which aired on ABC in 1986.

Scott Baio is best known for the television roles Chachi Arcola on *Happy Days,* Charles on *Charles in Charge,* and Dr. Jack Stewart on *Diagnosis: Murder.* Baio has appeared in several other, short-lived sitcoms, including *Baby Talk* and *Rewind.* In addition, he has starred in the award-winning independent films *Very Mean Men, Face to Face,* and *The Bread, My Sweet.* In 2005, Baio joined *Arrested Development* for the FOX sitcom's third season as Bob Loblaw, the Bluth's family lawyer.

Michele Balan (www.michelebalan.com) is a stand-up comedian who was a runner-up on NBC's *Last Comic Standing.* She has performed on Comedy Central and in top comedy clubs, theaters, and festivals and on cruises all over the country. She has shared the stage with Kathy Najimy, Jennifer Holiday, Taylor Dane, Harvey Fierstein, Bruce Vilanch, and Nell Carter, among others.

Rick Barber is a top-rated radio talk show host on 850 KOA in Denver.

Chris Barish is the owner of the New York nightclub Light. He is the son of the producer Keith Barish, the founder of Planet Hollywood, and socialite Ann Barish.

Arj Barker (www.arj.barker.com) is a comedian and actor who cowrote and currently stars in the off-Broadway hit *The Marijuanalogues*. He has performed in sixteen countries and has appeared on television on *The Late Show with David Letterman*, *Late Night with Conan O'Brien*, *The Tonight Show with Jay Leno*, *Jimmy Kimmel Live*, *Real Time with Bill Maher*, and two half-hour specials on Comedy Central.

Iran (Blade) Barkley is a five-time world boxing champion who holds five different title belts in four weight divisions. He is the only fighter to win twice against Tommy Hearns. After his retirement, he formed Boxers for Boxers to reform the sport. He is also active in Foundation Blade, an organization he founded where he speaks to children to help them deal with various problems in their lives.

Greer Barnes is a nationally touring stand-up comedian who has appeared on *The Late Show with David Letterman*, *Chappelle's Show*, *Last Call with Carson Daly*, and the film *For the Love of the Game*.

Todd Barry (www.toddbarry.com) is a nationally known stand-up comedian whose credits include *Late Show with David Letterman*, *Late Night with Conan O'Brien*, *Comedy Central Presents: Todd Barry*, *Last Call with Carson Daly*, *Jimmy Kimmel Live*, *Dr. Katz, Professional Therapist*, as well as the films *Road Trip*, *Pootie Tang* and *Tomorrow Night*.

Jacqueline Beaulieu is a model, ballerina, and actress who has appeared on the cover of several national magazines.

Richard Belzer (www.richardbelzer.com) is a veteran stand-up comedian, actor, talk show host, and author who is currently best known for his acerbic character Detective John Munch on *Law &*

Order: Special Victims Unit, which he first portrayed on NBC's critically acclaimed drama series *Homicide: Life on the Streets* for seven seasons. Film credits include *Man on the Moon, Species II, Get on the Bus, Girl 6, A Very Brady Sequel, North, The Bonfire of the Vanities,* and *The Big Picture.*

Ross Bennett (www.rossbennett.com) has been a fixture on the New York comedy club circuit for more than two decades and is a graduate of West Point. His television credits include Comedy Central, *Evening at the Improv, Comic Strip Live, Comedy Tonight, Entertainment Tonight,* and *Stand Up, Stand Up.*

Sid Bernstein is an internationally known concert promoter and legend recognized for bringing the Beatles, the Rolling Stones, the Kinks, the Moody Blues, Herman's Hermits, and many other English bands to the United States to perform. He also produced and promoted concerts by Elvis Presley, Laura Nyro, Blood Sweat and Tears, the Young Rascals, Sly and the Family Stone, and many others.

Dr. Laurie Betito (www.drlaurie.com) is a Canadian sex therapist, psychologist, lecturer, and television and radio host best known for her top-rated call-in show *Passion,* which has aired on CJAD 800 in Montreal since 1999.

Billy Bingo (www.billybingo.com) was a New York firefighter for twenty years and now performs stand-up comedy full time. He performs at Carolines on Broadway and is a frequent guest on the *Joey Reynolds Show* on WOR-AM radio in New York.

Mike Birbiglia (www.birbigs.com, www.myspace.com/birbigs) is a nationally known comic who has appeared on *The Late Show with David Letterman* in addition to having two Comedy Central Specials. His CD "Two Drink Mike" is currently in stores.

Geno Bisconte (www.ginobisconte.com) is a nationally touring comic and current spokesperson for the Delaware Lottery. His other film and television credits include *Behind Bars, Cross Fire III—Destiny, Arrest and Trial, Around Town,* and *Ben Guyatt's Comedy Kitchen.*

Dena Blizzard (www.denablizzard.com) is a stand-up comedian who has performed at Catch a Rising Star, the Improv, Gotham Comedy Club in New York, and the Comedy Stop in Atlantic City and Las Vegas. She is the winner of the 2004 Ladies of Laughter "New Talent" title and was voted one of the top ten stand-ups in 2005.

Mike Bocchetti (www.mikebocchetti.com) is a stand-up comedian and actor whose credits include the independent feature film *Chooch,* as well as appearances on *The Tonight Show with Jay Leno, The Howard Stern Show,* and NBC's *Last Comic Standing.* He can also be seen regularly in top clubs and numerous commercials, and has appeared in the USA Network hit show *New York.*

Bill Boggs (www.billboggs.com) is a four-time Emmy Award-winning TV host who has been a major figure in the lifestyle, food, travel, consumer, sports, news, and celebrity reporting arenas for more than 25 years, and is host of the New York based *Midday Live with Bill Boggs* and *Weekend Today in New York* (along with the long-running Food Network hit, *Bill Boggs' Corner Table*).

Paul Borghese is an actor, producer, and director who played the baseball legend Yogi Berra in the film *61,* which was directed by Billy Crystal. His other credits include *Find Me Guilty, Law & Order, Without a Trace, Little Manhattan, Searching for Bobby D,* and *Transamerica,* among others. He also produced and directed at television pilot for the Food Channel called *Dinner with the Foodfellas—An Invitation You Can't Refuse.*

Eddie Brill (www.eddiebrill.com) is the audience warm-up and talent coordinator for *The Late Show with David Letterman.* Besides *Letterman,* he has been the audience warm-up for *The Dana*

Carvey Show, Madigan Men, This Is Your Life, and *Saved by the Bell* and has appeared in numerous films.

Gina Brillon is a nationally touring comic who has been seen on Comedy Central, SI TV, and appeared at The Underground Coors Light and Jack Daniels Comedy Festivals.

Dick Capri is a veteran comedian who has performed in every major entertainment medium, including film, television, Broadway, as well as appearing at leading nightclubs and resorts. He has worked with such major stars as Tom Jones, Liza Minnelli, and Frank Sinatra.

Drew Carey (www.myspace.com/drewcarey) is an actor and comedian best-known for his hit ABC sitcom *The Drew Carey Show.* He also appeared in the 2005 film *The Aristocrats* and is a longtime regular on the hit game show *Whose Line Is It Anyway?*, among many other credits.

Jimmy Carr (www.jimmycarr.com) has been featured in his own Comedy Central special and has also appeared on *The Tonight Show with Jay Leno* and *Late Night with Conan O'Brien.*

Sarit Catz (www.princessofcomedy.com) has been a writer-producer on *Coach, Full House, Soul Man, Talk to Me, The Crew, Café Americain, Honey, I Shrunk the Kids,* and other television series and has won three Writer's Guild of America Awards. As a stand-up comic, she has performed at such top comedy clubs as the Comic Strip, Stand-Up New York, Gotham Comedy Club, the Improv, and many others.

Dick Cavett is an American talk show icon who began his career as a stand-up comedian and later as a writer for *The Tonight Show Starring Johnny Carson.* From 1969 until 1996, he was the host of his own talk show in various formats and on various television and radio networks for which he was nominated for eleven Emmy Awards and won three.

Chadeo is a comedian and actor whose credits include *Law & Order*, *Good Day Live*, and the Discovery Channel.

Greg Charles (www.dailycomedy.com) is the director of publicity at Carolines on Broadway in New York, where he also performs and hosts the monthly comedy showcase *The Greg Charles Show*.

Frank Chindamo (www.funlittlemovies.com) is the president and chief creative officer of Fun Little Movies, the largest content producer of comedy films on cellular phones.

Bruce Christensen is an actor, comedian, and impressionist who performs as a Conan O'Brien look-alike under the name "Clonan."

Johnny Cigar is the host of *Johnny Cigar's Traveling Saloon*, a monthly live radio show.

John (Cha-Cha) Ciarcia, is a television and film actor who is known as "The Mayor of Little Italy." He currently plays Albie Cianflone on *The Sopranos*. He is also cohost of *The Wiseguy Show* on Sirius Satellite Radio with *Sopranos* costars Vincent Pastore and Joe Rigano.

Samantha Cole (www.samanthacole.com) is an internationally known singer, songwriter, *Playboy* model and actress.

Felicia Collins (www.feliciacollins.com) is currently the lead guitarist in Paul Shaffer's band on *The Late Show with David Letterman*. Before that, she played guitar in Cindy Lauper's band.

Pat Cooper is a legendary nationally known comedian who has appeared on many stages, from comedy clubs to major theaters, including the legendary Copacabana, Westbury Music Theater,

Trump Castle, Caesar's Palace, the MGM Grand Hotel, and Trop World.

Professor Irwin Corey is a legendary comedian who has been affectionately known as "The World's Most Foremost Authority" for more than sixty years. He first gained prominence on the talk shows of Steve Allen, Jack Paar, Johnny Carson, and Ed Sullivan. He also performed on the *Martha Ray Show, Sergeant Bilko*, and the Andy Griffith, Andy Williams, and Doc Bernard Hughes TV shows, and has appeared on the talk shows of Dick Cavett, Merv Griffin, Mike Douglas, Pat Boone, Joe Franklin, and David Letterman. His film appearances include *Jack, I'm Not Rappaport*, and *The Curse of the Jade Scorpion*.

Gene Cornish was an original member of the rock band The Young Rascals.

Pete Correale (www.petecorreale.com) is a nationally touring comedian who has been featured at both the Montreal and Aspen Comedy Festivals. He has appeared on Comedy Central's *Premium Blend, Shorties Watchin' Shorties*, and *Tough Crowd with Colin Quinn* and has had numerous appearances on *Last Call with Carson Daly*, MTV, VHI, and *The Tonight Show with Jay Leno*. He can also be heard every weekday afternoon on Sirius Satellite Radio, where he is the cohost with Jim Breuer on *Breuer Unleashed*.

Tom Cotter (www.tomcotter.com) is a nationally known stand-up comic whose credits include NBC's *The Tonight Show with Jay Leno*, CBS's *Late Late Show with Craig Kilborn*, Comedy Central's *Comedy Central Presents Tom Cotter, Premium Blend, Two Drink Minimum, Short Attention Span Theater, Stand-Up, Stand-Up*, The Metro Channel's *New Joke City with Robert Klein* and A&E's *Evening at the Improv*.

Norm Crosby, "the Master of Malaprops," is among the most recognized and widely quoted comedians in show business. For many years, Crosby has been one of the busiest "name" comedians in the nation's top night clubs, theaters, and casino showrooms, as well as on top television variety, talk, and game shows. Crosby also starred as himself in the comedy series *The Boys*, which premiered to critical acclaim for the Showtime cable network in 1989.

Vince Curatola is an acclaimed actor who has portrayed the character of the New York mob boss Johnny Sack on *The Sopranos* since 1999. Other recent credits include the 2005 comedy *Fun with Dick and Jane* and the upcoming film *Karma: Confessions and Holi* with Naomi Campbell.

Errol Dante is an internationally recognized singer whose repertoire ranges from Broadway and contemporary rock to America's favorite standards and a large range of international favorites, including Spanish, French, Italian, Hebrew and Yiddish.

Tony Darrow is an actor who currently plays "Larry Boy" Baresi on *The Sopranos* and has starred in numerous films, including *Goodfellas*, *Analyze This*, and *Mickey Blue Eyes*, among many others. He also starred in a television pilot for the Food Channel called *Dinner with the Foodfellas—An Invitation You Can't Refuse*.

Jim David (www.jimdavid.com) is a nationally known comic who had his own special *Comedy Central Presents Jim David*, and has been seen on *Tough Crowd with Colin Quinn*, *Out on the Edge*, Comedy Central's *USO Tour*, ABC's *The View*, NBC *Comedy Showcase* with Louie Anderson, A&E's *Evening at the Improv*, VH1's *Fools for Love*, NBC's *Dateline*, *Star Search*, and *Last Call*, besides serving as a "comedy consultant" on Bravo's *Queer Eye for the Straight Guy* and *Greatest Things about Being*.

Doug Dechert is an award-winning journalist whose work regularly appears in the *New York Post*'s "Page Six," *Gotham Magazine*, and *Hamptons Magazine*.

Jessica Delfino (www.jessydelfino.blogspot.com) is an award-winning stand-up comedian and writer whose credits include ABC's *Good Morning America*, radio's *The Opie & Anthony Show* and the Sundance Channel. She also wrote all the songs to Morgan Spurlock's film *What Would Jesus Buy?*

William DeMeo is an actor and producer whose credits include playing Jason Molinaro on *The Sopranos* and appearances in such films as *Boss of Bosses*, *Analyze That*, *Wannabes*, *Unmade Man* and *Searching for Bobby D.*, among others.

Jamie DeRoy (www.jamiederoy.com) has been declared "the Fairy Godmother of Cabaret" because she has helped so many performers in the cabaret world. A gifted singer-comedienne, DeRoy has appeared as Joan Rivers's opening act in New York and Los Angeles and has headlined at every major club in New York. She has also enjoyed successful engagements at Caesar's Palace, Showboat, and Trump Plaza in Atlantic City, and the Sahara in Lake Tahoe.

Wendy Diamond (www.animalfair.com) is an internationally known media personality, television host, publisher of *Animal Fair* magazine, and pet contributor for NBC's *Today* show on NBC. She is the host of *Relationship Rehab* on E! Style Networks and is also a consulting producer and host on *Animal Planet*. She has been featured in *Time* magazine, the *New York Times*, *People*, and the *New Yorker*, as well as on *The View* and *Oprah*, among other places.

Roger Dreyer (www.fantasmagic.com) is a nationally acclaimed magician and the founder and CEO of Fantasma Magic in New York.

Dean Edwards (www.deanedwards.net) is a nationally known stand-up comedian and actor who appeared on *Saturday Night*

Live from 2001 until 2003. His other credits include, *The Sopranos, Def Comedy Jam, Premium Blend, Showtime at the Apollo,* MTV's *Where My Dawgs At* and the film *Tina & Tony's Wedding,* among others.

Brett Eidman (www.bretteidman.com) is a comedian and a radio personality known for his comedy song parodies that are played on FM, XM, and Sirius radio. He's also been seen in sketches on *SNL,* and has a new CD entitled, *What's So F*ckin' Funny,* on the Uproar Label.

Chris Elliott is a nationally known comedian, actor, and writer who got his start playing an assortment of oddball characters on NBC's *Late Night with David Letterman* in the early 1980s. His other television credits include *Saturday Night Live, Dilbert,* and his own sitcom *Get a Life.* Film credits include *There's Something about Mary, Groundhog Day, The Abyss, Scary Movie 2, Onassis Jones, Manhunter,* and others. He is the author of *Daddy's Boy* and *The Shroud of the Thacker.*

Kent Emmons (www.martinitimeradio.com) is the CEO of National Lampoon Radio and of Studio Funny Films. Besides hosting the hugely popular program *Martini Time* on WQUN-AM radio in Connecticut, he is the former manager of singer-songwriter Bertie Higgins, who had the hit single "Key Largo."

Susie Essman (www.susieessman.com) is a nationally known comedian and actress who has appeared in numerous television programs, including her own half-hour special HBO's *One Night Stand, The Tonight Show with Jay Leno, Politically Incorrect,* and *Law & Order.* She also appeared in the off-Broadway hit *The Vagina Monologues* and can be seen in the recurring role of Susie Greene in Larry David's smash-hit HBO series *Curb Your Enthusiasm.* Her film credits include *Volcano, The Siege,* and *Keeping the Faith,* among others.

Howard Feller is a stand-up comedian best known as the side-kick to John Stewart on MTV. His other television and film credits include *The Invisible Man, Dellaventura, Friday Night, Caroline's Comedy Hour, MTV Half-Hour Comedy Show, Nothing Upstairs, Awakenings,* and *Radio Days.*

John Femia (groups.msn.com/thestandipsasylum) first came to the public eye in the early 1980s when he costarred with Sarah Jessica Parker in the hit television series *Square Pegs.* He currently performs stand-up regularly at clubs around the country and is also a producer and founder of *Stand-Ups Asylum* and the host for Comedy Express TV.

Jordon Ferber (www.myspace.com/jordonferber) is a stand-up comedian and actor who regularly performs in New York and around the country. He was also featured on the NBC reality series *Last Comic Standing* during its first season.

Adam Ferrara (www.adamferrara.com) is a nationally known comedian and actor nominated for two American Comedy Awards for best stand-up. His television credits include ABC's *The Job, Law & Order,* and multiple appearances on Comedy Central, including two half-hour specials, *The Tonight Show with Jay Leno, The Late Show with David Letterman, The View, Politically Incorrect, The Rosie O'Donnell Show,* and *The Late, Late Show with Craig Kilborn.*

Jon Fisch (www.johnfisch.com and www.myspace.com/johnfisch) is a stand-up comic and monologist who has been seen on Comedy Central's *Premium Blend* and has contributed to the *Onion's* "Say Something" column. He appears regularly in New York City at the Comic Strip Live, Carolines on Broadway, and Gotham Comedy Club.

Buddy Flip (www.buddyflip.com) is a nationally known stand-up comedian who also manages New York Comedy Club and teaches classes on stand-up comedy.

Tom Fontana (www.tomfontana.com) is an internationally known award-winning television writer and producer whose numerous credits include *St. Elsewhere, Homicide, Life on the Street, Oz, The Beat, The Jury,* and *Bedford Diaries,* all of which he either produced, wrote, or created.

Karith Foster (www.karithfoster.com) has performed in all the major comedy clubs in New York, including Carolines on Broadway, the Comic Strip, New York Comedy Club, and Stand-Up New York, as well as in Los Angeles clubs the Laugh Factory, the Improv, and the Comedy Store. Her television appearances include Comedy Central's *Premium Blend,* NBC's *Last Comic Standing, The Original Showtime at the Apollo, Comedy TKO, The Ricki Lake Show,* and *She's So Funny* on Canada's National Women's Television Network

Bethenny Frankel (www.bethennyfrankel.com) is the owner of Bethenny Bakes, a low-fat, wheat-dairy-and-egg-free cookie company in New York City and a former runner-up on Martha Stewart's reality series *The Apprentice.*

Joe Franklin is a radio and television legend whose *Joe Franklin Show* has been on for a record forty-plus years. Franklin has been featured in newspapers such as the *New York Times, Newsday,* the *Wall Street Journal,* the *New York Post,* the *Village Voice,* and the *Newark Star-Ledger,* and in magazines such as *Parade* and the *New Yorker.* He has also been a featured segment on ABC's *Day One* and has appeared in movies such as *Ghostbusters, Broadway Danny Rose,* and *Manhattan.* He can currently be heard on *Joe Franklin's Memory Lane* on WOR-AM radio in New York and on Bloomberg Radio.

Montgomery Frazier (www.m3imagegroup.com) is an internationally known image consultant who heads up the M3 Image Group in New York and whose work can frequently be seen on MTV.

Mickey Freeman is a legendary stand-up comedian and actor best known for his role as Private Zimmerman on *The Phil Silvers Show*. He's a regular on *The Joey Reynolds Show* and a longtime active member of the New York Friars Club.

Bobby Funaro (www.hbo.com/sopranos/cast/character/eugene_pontacorvo.shtml *and* www.robertfunaro.com) is an actor-director who has appeared regularly on *The Sopranos* as Eugene Pontecorvo.

Jeff Garlin is a nationally known comedian-actor who currently costars and executive produces the critically acclaimed HBO series *Curb Your Enthusiasm* and before that spent three seasons on NBC's *Mad about You* in the role of Marvin. Other film and television appearances include *Full Frontal*, *Daddy Day Care*, *Austin Powers: The Spy Who Shagged Me*, *Bounce*, *Everybody Loves Raymond*, *The Late Show with David Letterman*, *The Daily Show with John Stewart*, and *Late Night with Conan O'Brien*.

Steven Garrin (www.videoactiveprod.com) is the executive producer of VideoActive Productions and the founder of the highly acclaimed VoiceWorks voice-over workshop. He is currently a licensing partner of Joe Franklin's Comedy Club and just finished directing, recording, and editing the Broadway legend Carol Channing reading her autobiography *Just Lucky, I Guess*.

Joey Gay (www.joeygay.com) is an actor-comedian who has performed at Carolines on Broadway, Comedy Village, and the Laugh Factory. Television and film credits include *Law & Order*, *Law &Order: Special Victims Unit*, *Deadline*, *Close Strangers*, and MTV's *Damage Control*.

Adam Gilad is the program director for National Lampoon Radio in Los Angeles, an online dating expert, and the author of *Net to Bed/Net to Wed: How to Attract the Woman of Your Dreams, for a Night, for a Lifetime, or Anything in Between*, which he wrote under the name Grant Adams. Gilad is also a screenwriter of many movies including *Not in This Town* and was the executive producer of *The Ron Clark Story*. In addition, he has written over twenty animated television episodes and was featured in the ABC reality series *How to Get the Guy*.

Greg Giraldo (www.greggiraldo.com) is a nationally known comedian who has starred in his own ABC sitcom *Common Law*. He has also appeared on NBC's *Late Night with Conan O'Brien*, *Last Call with Carson Daly*, *The View*, *The Late, Late Show with Craig Kilborn*, and *Politically Incorrect*.

Judy Gold (www.judygold.com) is an Emmy Award–winning actress and comedian who currently stars in the critically acclaimed off-Broadway show *25 Questions for a Jewish Mother*. She is also the host of HBO's *At the Multiplex with Judy Gold* and also hosted Comedy Central's *100 Greatest Stand-Ups of All Time*. Her stand-up specials include *Comedy Central Presents: Judy Gold*, Comedy Central's *Tough Crowd Stands Up*, and an HBO half-hour special, which received a Cable Ace Award. Gold won two Emmy Awards for writing and producing *The Rosie O'Donnell Show* and was nominated twice for the American Comedy Awards' Funniest Female Stand-Up Comedian. She appeared in the film *The Aristocrats* and has also appeared on *Law & Order*, *Law & Order: Special Victim's Unit*, *The View*, *The Tonight Show with Jay Leno*, and *Late Night with Conan O'Brien*.

Julie Goldman (www.juliegoldman.com) can be seen as a part of the irregular series Laughing Liberally and is LOGO's new sketch comedy show produced by Rosie O'Donnell called *The Big Gay Show*.

Gilbert Gottfried (www.gilbertgottfried.com) is a nationally known stand-up comedian-actor, often heard on *The Howard Stern Show*. His film credits include Disney's *Aladdin*, *Problem Child*, and *The Aristocrats*. Television appearances include all major talk shows, including *The Late Show with David Letterman*, *The Tonight Show with Jay Leno*, and the voice of the duck in the AFLAC commercials. Material from his CD *Dirty Jokes* is featured in this book.

Sal the Stockbroker Governale (www.horsetoothjackass.com) is an American radio personality and comedian who currently works as a writer on *The Howard Stern Show*. In addition to writing for the show, he also made *Supertwink: The Movie* for *Howard Stern on Demand*, and is currently performing stand-up at various clubs.

Marion Grodin is a nationally touring stand-up comedian, producer and actress who has appeared on NBC's *Late Night with Conan O'Brien*, Metro Channel's *New Joke City with Robert Klein*, *Inside Edition*, *The Charles Grodin Show* and ABC's *The View*. She is actor Charles Grodin's daughter.

Gary Gulman (www.garygulman.com) was a costar of HBO's *Tourgasm* with Dane Cook and has appeared on *Last Comic Standing*, *The Tonight Show with Jay Leno*, and *Late Show with David Letterman*.

Allan Havey (www.allanhavey.com) is a veteran stand-up comedian and actor. He has appeared regularly on *The Late Show with David Letterman*. He also created and hosted *Night after Night* for three years on Comedy Central. He recently starred in the Fox sitcom *Free Ride*, as well as *Curb Your Enthusiasm*, and *Punk'd*.

Vic Henley (www.vichenley.com) is a nationally known stand-up comedian and writer who has appeared on *The Tonight Show with Jay Leno*, *The Late Show with David Letterman* and Comedy Central's *Tough Crowd with Colin Quinn* where he was also featured in his own 2005 half-hour stand-up special. He is the author of *Things You'd Never Expect a Southerner to Say* and co-author of *Games Rednecks Play* with Jeff Foxworthy.

Tim Homayoon (www.thatcomedyguy.com) is a nationally known stand-up comedian and writer whose credits include appearing on MTV, NBC and Comedy Central, as well as writing for *Saturday Night Live's Weekend Update*. He regularly performs in New York at Caroline's on Broadway, Stand-Up New York and The Laugh Factory.

Helen Hong (www.helenhong.com) is a stand-up comedian who regularly appears in New York at Carolines on Broadway, Gotham Comedy Club, and the Comic Strip. She also provides commentary for E! Entertainment television and was formerly a producer for *Live with Regis and Kelly* and *The Jane Pauley Show*.

John Hoyt is an actor/producer who has appeared in many films, like Abel Ferrara's *The Funeral*, *Bullets Over Broadway*, *Die Hard: With A Vengeance*, *Basketball Diaries*, and *Carlito's Way*. He also won the award for Best Actor at the NY International Film Festival for his portrayal of a huge Woody Allen in the award-winning short film *I Am Woody*.

Frankie Hudak (www.frankiehudak.com) is a stand-up comedian and actor who hosts a monthly comedy series for Continental Airlines called *What Just Happened*.

Adam Hunter (www.adamhunter.com) is a nationally touring comedian. He can be seen on three VH1 specials: *Robbing the Cradle*, *Brittney vs. Christina*, and *16 Candles: Behind the Movie*. He also just filmed the comedy show *Funny Is Funny*, had a guest starring role on *Yes, Dear*, and has appeared on *The Late, Late Show with Craig Kilborne* and Comedy Central's *Premium Blend*. In addition, Hunter was the subject of the MTV show *True Life: I Am a Comic* and *Facebiters*.

Ice-T (www.icet.com) is a multitalented actor and musician who currently plays Detective Odafin "Fin" Tutola on *Law & Order: Special Victims Unit*. His film credits include *New Jack City, Ricochet, Johnny Mnemonic, Tank Girl,* and *Trespass*. He is also the author of *The Ice Opinion*.

Duncan Jay (www.myspace.com/duncanjay) is a stand-up comedian who performs regularly at comedy clubs in New York and throughout the country.

Ron Jeremy (www.ronjeremy.com and www.barnaclebillthesailor. com) is an internationally known porn star–actor whose career encompasses more than 1,600 films, over a hundred of which he directed. Throughout his career, Jeremy has broken into mainstream Hollywood through many parts in studio and independent films, as well as by serving as a consultant in *Boogie Nights and Nine½ Weeks*.

Richard Johnson is the editor of "Page Six," the notorious, no-holds-barred daily gossip column in the *New York Post*, a position he has held since 1985. He is a graduate of Yale.

Baird Jones is an art curator who is featured regularly in the *New York Post* "Page Six."

Will Jordan is a nationally known comedian-impressionist-actor-motivational speaker who is best known for his uncanny impression of Ed Sullivan and his ability to look like the people he impersonates. Television credits include *The Ed Sullivan Show, The Tonight Show Starring Johnny Carson, The Mike Douglas Show, The Jack Paar Show,* and *The Copycats*.

Alli Joseph (www.allijoseph.com) is a television host, reporter, writer, and producer. She uncovered the hottest trends in restaurants, gadgets, cuisine, kitchen design, diets, and much more on *What's Hot, What's Cool,* a Food Network show. She has also worked as a television producer and reporter for USA Network, CBS News, VH1, and TNT, among other places.

Cory Kahaney (www.corykahaney.com) was one of the five finalists on the original *Last Comic Standing* and has had her own stand-up special on Comedy Central. She was a regular on *Tough Crowd with Colin Quinn* and has also appeared on *The View, Last Call with Carson Daly,* and *Politically Incorrect.* She performs regularly at clubs in New York City and across the country and was featured on Donald Trump's *The Apprentice.*

Arie Kaplan (www.arikaplan.com) is a writer, comedian, and frequent contributor to *Mad* magazine. He is also the author of *Masters of the Comic Book Universe Revealed.*

Ellen Karis (www.ellenkaris.com) is a stand-up comedian who appears at comedy clubs in New York City, Long Island and New Jersey, and has been featured on ABCNews.com's *Good Humor* and appeared on *The Sopranos,* among other credits.

Robert Kelly (www.robertkelly.com) is a favorite at comedy clubs and colleges nationwide who was a costar in Dane Cook's HBO series *Tourgasm.* His other television credits include Comedy Central's *Premium Blend,* NBC's *The Carson Daly Show,* Comedy Central's *Tough Crowd with Colin Quinn,* and VH1's *Awesomely Oversexed* and MTV. He also guest starred on ABC's sitcom *The Job* with Denis Leary, and appeared as a detective playing opposite Vincent D'Onofrio on NBC's *Law & Order: Criminal Intent.*

Bryan Kennedy is a stand-up comedian in New York who currently hosts New Class Clowns at Caroline's on Broadway.

King is a noted New York nightlife impresario who has held numerous longtime associations with such legendary clubs as the

Copacabana, Bowery Bar, the new Studio 54, Plaid, Limelight, Bungalow 8, and Tuesday Night at Life.

Alan Kirschenbaum is a television producer and writer who created the hit CBS sitcom *Yes, Dear*. His other credits include being the executive producer of *Coach* and a writer on *Dear John*, *Anything But Love*, *Stark Raving Mad*, and *Down the Shore*.

Jessica Kirson (www.jessiccakirson.com) is a stand-up comic who has been featured on various television shows, including Comedy Central's *Premium Blend* and *Fresh Faces*, Nickelodeon's *Sixth in the Suburbs*, Noggins *LOL*, VH1's *Awesomely Bad Hair* and *Awesomely Bad Love Songs*, Oxygen's *Can You Tell?*, Bravo's *The Great Things about Being*, the Women's Television Network's *She's So Funny*, and NBC's *Last Comic Standing* and *Last Call with Carson Daly*.

Dave Konig (www.davekonig.com) is an Emmy Award-winning stand-up comedian, television personality and actor whose credits include hosting the HBO comedy series *Hardcore TV*, *Subway Q&A* on New York's Metro Channel, and playing DJ Vince Fontaine in the '90s revival of *Grease* on Broadway. He currently performs at comedy clubs around New York and is the co-host of *Speak Now or Forever Hold Your Peace* on Sirius Satellite Radio with his wife Susan.

Lynne Koplitz is an accomplished stand-up comedian and television personality who co-hosted Sony's syndicated talk show *Life and Style* with Jules Asner, Kimora Lee Simmons, and Cynthia Garrett, as well as her own half-hour Comedy Central special *Comedy Presents with Lynne Koplitz*. In addition, she was the cohost of the comedy cooking show *How to Boil Water* on the Food Network and *Change of Heart*, the nationally syndicated relationship show. She has also appeared as a guest host on NBC's *Later*, had a development deal with NBC for her own sitcom, was a featured comedian on Comedy Central's *Premium Blend,* and guest-starred on NBC's *Extra and The Other Half.*

Kenny Kramer (www.kennykramer.com) is an internationally known stand-up comic who inspired the character of the same name on *Seinfeld.* He has been featured on *The Oprah Winfrey Show,* the *Today* show, *Dateline NBC, The Maury Povich Show,* CNN, *Entertainment Tonight,* CNBC, MSNBC, *Inside Edition, Access Hollywood,* and *Extra.*

Dr. Judith Kuriansky (www.sexualtherapy.com/therapists/jkurianski) is a clinical psychologist, sex therapist, and media personality. She hosts the call-in show *LovePhones,* which is based in New York and syndicated across the United States. She has appeared on television programs such as *Larry King Live, 48 Hours, Oprah,* and CNN's *TalkBackLive,* is the author of *The Complete Idiot's Guide to Tantric Sex* and *The Complete Idiot's Guide to a Healthy Relationship,* and is a contributor to *Penthouse* magazine.

Lisa Lampanelli (www.insultcomic.com) is the only performer to have ever appeared twice on *The Tonight Show with Jay Leno* within six weeks. Nicknamed "Comedy's Loveable Queen of Mean," she has also appeared on *Comedy Central's Weekends at the D.L.* Her headlining performance on the *Comedy Central Roast of Pamela Anderson* received national attention and she was the only female comedian invited to skewer Chevy Chase at the New York Friars Club Roast of Chevy Chase in 2002. Lampanelli has also taped several specials for VH1, MTV, and CMT, and was featured on the "Best Of" episode of Comedy Central's *Tough Crowd with Colin Quinn,* besides having film appearances in *Larry the Cable Guy: Health Inspector,* and *The Aristocrats.*

Johnny Lampert (www.johnnylampert.com) is considered one of the premier comedians in the country. He is a regular at New York's and Los Angeles' best comedy clubs, including the Comic Strip and the Improv. He has also made numerous television appearances on MTV, A&E's *Caroline's Comedy Hour*, NBC's *Friday Night*, *HBO Comedy Showcase with Louie Anderson*, and Comedy Central's *Premium Blend*.

P.J. Landers is a stand-up comic and the owner of Comedy Village in New York.

Maureen Langan (www.maureenlangan.com) is a comedian and actress who performs at the top clubs in New York City, Atlantic City, and Las Vegas. She hosts a nationally syndicated morning radio show called *The Radio Ritas* and was formerly the entertainment reporter for *Bloomberg Business News*.

Artie Lange (www.artie-lange.com) is a nationally known comedian who is best known as the current sidekick to the radio shock jock Howard Stern. Heard every day on the radio and seen every night on Howard's E! Entertainment Television show, he was also one of the original nine cast members of *MADtv*. His other film and television appearances include *Dirty Work*, *Mystery Men*, *The Bachelor*, and the ABC sitcom *The Norm Show* with Norm McDonald.

David Lappin is the sales director for a large New York book publishing company. He is from Canada. His hobbies include reading, traveling, and having anxiety attacks. He has not appeared in the following movies: *Gone with the Wind*, *Casablanca*, or *Attack of the Fifty-Foot Woman*.

Neil Lasher is the vice president of promotion/marketing and artist relations for EMI Music Publishing in New York.

Ann Lee is a New York-based comedian originally from Asia who currently performs at such top New York comedy clubs as Caroline's on Broadway, the Improv, Joe Franklin's, and Gotham Comedy Club.

Jay Leslie is a singer-musician who was one of the original members of the rock group the Tokens, best known for their hit "The Lion Sleeps Tonight." He was also a former bass player for Sha-Na-Na.

Evelyn Liu (www.evelynliu.com) is an actress and fitness model who has appeared in ads for Nike, Pepsi, Vitamin Water, Mercedes-Benz, Victoria's Secret, and L'Oreal. She has also been seen as a nurse in over 100 episodes of the long-running CBS soap opera *As the World Turns.*

Danny Lobell (www.thecomical.com) is a stand-up comedian, radio host, and publisher of *The Comical,* a newspaper that is distributed to patrons of comedy clubs.

Dick Lord is an internationally known comedian who has played every major nightclub in the world. He also appeared on *The Merv Griffin Show* a record twenty-two times, as well *The Tonight Show Starring Johnny Carson,* besides having had his own special on ABC, his own show on Cinemax called *Cinemax Comics,* and serving as a creative consultant on *The Bobby Darrin Show.*

Kerri Louise (www.kerrilouise.com) is a stand-up comic who currently stars in the Women's Entertainment Network's *Two Funny* and was a finalist in the first season of NBC's *Last Comic Standing.* A regular at top comedy clubs throughout the country, she has appeared on NBC's *Access Hollywood* and *The Apprentice,* ABC's *The View,* Comedy Central, VH1, *20/20,* and *New Joke City,* as well as at the Montreal and Aspen Comedy Festivals.

Countess LuAnn (www.luanndelesseps.com) is a New York television personality who currently hosts her own show on WVH Hamptons TV called *The Countess Report* and was featured on WCBS-TV during the Hampton Classic, where she filed stories on a regular basis.

Eric Lyden (www.ericlyden.com) is a stand-up comedian who performs in New York City, New Jersey, and comedy clubs in the surrounding areas.

Todd Lynn (www.toddlynn.net) is a stand-up comic who has appeared four times on BET's *Comic View* and has written for Comedy Central's *Comic Groove*. His other TV credits include *Late Night with Conan O'Brien*, *The Late Show with David Letterman*, and Comedy Central's *Premium Blend*, among others.

Mario Macaluso (www.mariomacaluso.com) is an actor and a founding member of the Feast of San Gennaro, LA, and is a board member of the New York Comedy Film Festival. He works with many different charities from comedy fund-raisers to watching films with ill children.

April Macie (myspace.com/aprilmacie) is a nationally touring stand-up comic who appeared most recently on NBC's *Last Comic Standing*. In 2005, she performed at the Montreal Comedy Festival's *New Faces Show*.

Macio (www.maciotv.com) is a nationally known stand-up comedian and actor whose credits include *Chappelle's Show*, *Def Comedy Jam*, and the hit syndicated series *Uptown Comedy Club*, which he wrote and produced. He hosted NBC's *Later* and starred in his own self-titled television pilot *The Macio Show*, which was produced by Quincy Jones and David Saltzman. He has also appeared in commercials for Burger King, Pepsi, and AT&T, and has performed with Chris Rock, Damon Wayans, Wanda Sykes, and D. L. Hughley.

Tonia Madenford (www.screenaddiction.com) is a producer and director of feature films, music videos, and documentaries.

Lenny Marcus (www.lennymarcus.com) is a stand-up comedian and short filmmaker who has appeared at the Aspen and Montreal Comedy Festivals. His television credits include NBC's *Friday Night* and *Comedy Showcase with Louie Anderson*, as well as commercials for Wendy's, Marriott, and IBM.

Jorjeana Marie (www.jorjeanamarie.com) is a comedian and voice-over artist who is currently the host of American Movie Classic's *Date Night* and the star of the independent film *Indelible*. Voice-over clients range from Nickelodeon to American Express. Film credits include working with Alec Baldwin in *The Devil and Daniel Webster*, Peter Howitt in MGM's *Antitrust*, James Mangold in *Kate and Leopold*, and Dave Chapelle on *The Chapelle Show*.

Jackie "the Jokeman" Martling (www.jokeman.com) is a well-known radio personality, stand-up comedian, and comedy writer who was a longtime cast member and chief writer of the top-rated *Howard Stern Show*. He was featured as himself in the Paramount feature film *Private Parts* and is also well known for his joke books and CDs.

Jackie Mason is an internationally known, award-winning comedian-actor radio and television host who has had seven hit shows on Broadway. He has won a Tony Award, an Outer Critics Circle Award, and Ace Award, an Emmy Award, and a Grammy nomination. His other credits include the film *Caddyshack II* and the ABC sitcom *Chicken Soup*.

Joseph (Joe Brat) McBratney (www.curvez.com) is a private investigator in New York who specializes in matrimonial cases, corporate theft, and Internet crimes. He is also an accomplished actor who has appeared in many television shows and films, including *Parco P.I.* on Court TV, *Hitch*, and *The Interpreter*. In cyberspace, he is the star of *Joe Brat-Internet Detective*.

Moody McCarthy (www.moodymccarthy.com) is a nationally known stand-up comedian whose credits include *Jimmy Kimmel Live* and *Last Comic Standing*, among others.

Malachy McCourt (www.malachymccourt.com) is the internationally known author of seven books, including *A Monk Swimming* and *Malachy McCourt's History of Ireland*. In 2006, he ran for governor in New York on the Green Party ticket.

Jim McCue (www.jimmccue.com) is a nationally known comic who founded The Boston Comedy Festival.

Steven "Spanky" McFarlin is a published author, magazine columnist, recording artist, television writer, producer, and award-winning stand-up comedian. He has appeared on television in *ER*, *Profiler*, and *The Jenny McCarthy Show* and was featured in the 1998 film *Molly* costarring Elizabeth Shue.

Patrick McMullan (www.patrickmcmullan.com) is a leading celebrity photographer based in New York whose work appears regularly in his weekly *New York* magazine column "Party Lines," as well as in *Allure*, *Interview*, *Hamptons*, *Ocean Drive*, and *Gotham*, among others. He is also a contributing editor at *Vanity Fair* and his photography has been featured in publications worldwide, such as the *New York Times Magazine* and *Vogue*, and in international editions of *Harper's Bazaar*, *Details*, *Tatler*, and *Out*, among many others.

Russ Meneve (www.russmeneve.com) is a nationally touring comic whose numerous credits include NBC's *Late Night with Conan O'Brien*, *Last Call with Carson Daly*, *Last Comic Standing*, and *The Caroline Rhea Show*.

Marilyn Michaels (www.marilynmichaels.com) is a comedian and impressionist who is known to audiences by her countless appearances on television shows such as *Regis and Kathie Lee*, *Lifestyles with Robin Leach*, *Sally Jesse Raphael*, and the *Howard Stern Show*, among many others.

Maria Milito is a stand-up comic and popular radio personality on Q104.3-FM radio in New York.

Peter Miller (www.pmalitfilm.com), known as "the Literary Lion," has been an active film and literary manager for more than thirty years. He is the president of PMA Literary and Film Management, Inc. and Lion, Inc., which have successfully managed more than 1,000 books worldwide as well as dozens of motion picture and television properties. These include eleven *New York Times* best sellers and eleven films that Miller has managed or executive produced. Three of those films—*Goodbye, Miss Fourth of July, A Gift of Love,* and *Helter Skelter*—have been nominated for Emmy Awards.

Dave Mordal is a nationally known stand-up comic who has been seen on *Last Comic Standing* and *Tough Crowd* with Colin Quinn.

John Morrison (www.myspace.com/morrisongod) is a stand-up comedian and the producer of Morrison Motel.

Milt Moss is a comedian-entertainer who appeared on *The Merry Mailman Show*, a children's program that ran on WOR-TV in New York in the 1950s.

Kate Mulgrew (www.totallykate.com) is a veteran stage and screen actress best known for her portrayal of Captain Kathryn Janeway on the television series *Star Trek Voyager*. In 2003, she received an Outer Critics Circle Award nomination for Outstanding Lead Actress for her performance in *Tea at Five*, her critically acclaimed one-woman show about the life of Katharine Hepburn.

Arthur Nascarella is a nationally known actor who has appeared in over fifty movies and currently plays Carlo Gervasi on *The Sopranos*. His film credits include *Copland, He Got Game, Good-*

fellas, Kate & Leopold, Bamboozled, The Curse of the Jade Scorpion, 9/11, and most recently The Groomsmen.

Jesse Nash is an entertainment journalist and travel writer who has written for numerous publications, including the New York Post's "Page Six."

Julius R. Nasso is an internationally known Hollywood film producer whose credits include Enemy Hands, Narc, One Eyed King, Prince of Central Park, The Patriot, On Deadly Ground, and Out for Justice, among many others.

Dan Naturman (www.dannaturman.com) is a nationally known stand-up comedian who has appeared on The Late Show with David Letterman, Late Night with Conan O'Brien, and his own special on Comedy Central. He was also a finalist on NBC's Last Comic Standing.

Dante Nero is a comic who has appeared on Tough Crowd with Colin Quinn and The Dave Chapelle Show.

Chuck Nice (www.chucknice.com) is the co-host of The Radio Chick Show on 92.3 Free F.M. in New York and also appears regularly on VH1's Best Week Ever and WE Entertainment's Cinema Therapy.

Jim Norton (www.eatabullet.com) is a nationally known stand-up comic, radio personality and actor who played the recurring part of Rich on the HBO series Lucky Louie. He also appears regularly on radio on the Opie and Anthony Show and has been seen in such films as Spider Man and Jerry Seinfeld's Comedian. His television credits include numerous appearances on The Colin Quinn Show, Tough Crowd with Colin Quinn and Last Call with Carson Daily.

Nic Novicki (www.nicnovicki.com) is a stand-up comedian and performer who studied improvisational comedy at the Upright Citizens Brigade. His credits include a recurring role as Alfe on *Saturday Night Live*, VH-1's *Hundred Metal Moments*, and numerous independent films.

Patrice Oneal (www.patriceoneal.com) is a nationally known comedian-actor who regularly appears at major comedy clubs in New York and across the country. He has performed at the Aspen Comedy Arts Festival and the Just for Laughs Festival in Montreal. Television credits include FOX's *Arrested Development* and *The Jury*, NBC's *The Office*, *The Late Show with David Letterman*, *Late Night with Conan O'Brien*, and *Tough Crowd with Colin Quinn* on Comedy Central. He also had half-hour specials on Showtime, HBO, and Comedy Central. Film credits include *Shorties Watchin' Shorties*, *O'Grady High*, *The 25th Hour*, *In the Cut*, and *Head of State*. He is currently the host of *WebJunk* on VH1.

Ellen Orchid is a New York-based stand-up comedian.

Frankie Pace (www.frankiepace.com) is a plumber-turned-stand-up comedian who has worked alongside other comics such as Eddie Murphy, Jackie Martling, Bob Nelson, and Rosie O'Donnell. In addition, he has appeared on *Saturday Night Live*, *The Cosby Show*, *The Joan Rivers Show*, Cinemax, *Show-offs with Malcom Jamal Warner*, *Caroline's Comedy Hour*, and many numerous comedy shows and specials.

Vinny Parco is the star of *Parco P.I.* on Court TV and a nationally known private investigator.

Vincent Pastore (www.vincentpastore.net) is a film and television actor who is best known for the role of Salvatore "Big Pussy" Bonpensiero on *The Sopranos*. He has film credits ranging from *Goodfellas* to *Shark Tale* and is also the cohost of *The Wiseguy Show* with John Ciarcia and Joe Rigano on Sirius Satellite Radio.

Bernadette Pauley (www.bernadettepauley.com) is currently the host of the Bravo Channel's *War of the Wives* and has also appeared on Andy Tennant's television pilot The Wedding Album for FOX and Comedy Central's *Tough Crowd with Colin Quinn.*

Andy Peeke (www.myspace.com/peekester) is an actor, comedian, and model who regularly performs in New York at the Comedy Village and Gotham Comedy Club.

John Pinette (www.johnpinette.com) is a nationally known stand-up comedian and actor who until recently played Edna Turnblad in the Broadway musical *Hairspray*. He was named Stand-Up Comedian of the Year by the American Comedy Awards in 1999 and received a Gemini Award nomination for his televised performance at the Montreal Comedy Festival in 2000. A regular on *The Tonight Show with Jay Leno* and *The View*, Pinette's other film and television credits include *Dear God, Duets, Junior, Seinfeld,* and *The Pusher.*

Jeff "Fat Rat Bastard" Pirrami (www.heyfattboy.com) is a stand-up comedian and has appeared with Frankie Valli, Charlie Daniels, and Ray Charles. He has appeared in comedy clubs throughout the country, such as in Las Vegas and Atlantic City.

Tommy Pooch, also known as the "unofficial mayor of South Beach, Florida," is a nightlife impresario in New York and South Beach known best in New York for Spo-Dee-O-Dee and in South Beach for many celebrity parties and gatherings.

Johnny Podell (www.podelltalent.com), featured in *New York Magazine*, is considered one of the top music agents in the world. He is the president and CEO of Podell Talent Agency in New York, one of the world's largest music talent representation agencies. The agency's clients include Alice Cooper, the Allman Brothers Band, Cyndi Lauper, Erasure, Gavin DeGraw, Gregg Allman & Friends, Jill Sobule, Peter Gabriel, Sammy Hagar, Silvertide, and Van Halen, among others.

Paul Provenza is a nationally known stand-up comedian, actor and television host who directed the hit 2005 film *The Aristocrats*.

Stacy Prussman (www.stacyprussman.com) tours internationally on the stand-up comedy circuit after years of working professionally in theater, television, and film. She is best known for playing the lead role of Dori Grossman in the long-running off-Broadway hit *Grandma Sylvia's Funeral* and starring in the award-winning independent film *Glam-Trash*.

Richard Pryor Jr. is the oldest son of the comedy legend Richard Pryor and an accomplished stand-up comedian and actor in his own right, having appeared at the Comedy Store in Los Angeles and other comedy clubs throughout the nation. He is currently at work on the one-man show *Call Me Richard* and an autobiography.

Colin Quinn (www.colinquinn.com) is a nationally known comedian whose television credits include his own show on Comedy Central *Tough Crowd with Colin Quinn*, MTV's *Remote Control*, and *Saturday Night Live*, where he was the anchor of "Weekend Update" for two and a half seasons. Film credits include *Comedian* with Jerry Seinfeld, *Married to the Mob*, and *Crocodile Dundee II*. Theater credits include his Broadway show *Colin Quinn: An Irish Wake*.

Louis Ramey is a comedian who currently stars on Nickelodeon's The *Nick @ Nite Road Crew*. His other credits include *The View*, *Last Comic Standing*, *The Tonight Show with Jay Leno*, and *Tough Crowd with Colin Quinn*, among many others. He has also performed as an opening act for Ray Charles, Whitney Houston, Smokey Robinson, Isaac Hayes, and Donna Summer.

Mason Reese is a former child actor who has appeared in more than seventy-five commercials, won seven Cleo Awards, and once appeared on the cover of *TV Guide*.

Aubrey Reuben is the theater critic for *15minutesmagazine.com* and a celebrity photographer whose work regularly appears in the *New York Post*, *Playbill*, Playbill.com, and *Playbill National Magazine*. His column "Aubrey's Broadway" also appears in the *Hampton Sheet*. He is also one of the eighteen profiles in *On Broadway Men Still Wear Hats* by Robert Simonson.

Joey Reynolds is the host of *The Joey Reynolds Show* on WOR-AM radio in New York. Considered to be one of the most creative persons in the United States, he was inducted into the Rock 'n' Roll Hall of Fame for his accomplishments in radio, television, and music. Reynolds also worked for 20th Century Fox, was instrumental in the *Star Wars* marketing program, and headed a company for the singer Wayne Newton for two years.

Daniella Rich is a stand-up comedian who has performed at Carolines on Broadway and other comedy clubs in New York and Los Angeles, as well as in the Hamptons Comedy Festival and the New York Underground Comedy Festival. She is the daughter of the socialite Denise Rich.

Denise Rich is an acclaimed New York socialite and composer who has written songs for artists such as Diana Ross, Celine Dion, and Donna Summer, among many others. She is also the founder of the G&P Foundation, which raises money to fight cancer, in honor of her daughter Gabrielle, who died of the disease at the age of twenty-six.

Marty Richards is a Tony Award–winning Broadway and film producer whose credits include *Chicago*, *Fort Apache the Bronx*, *The Shining*, *The Boys from Brazil*, and *Some of My Best Friends Are*, *Sweeny Todd*, *La Cage Aux Folles*, *A Doll's Life*, and *On the Twentieth Century*, among many others.

Joe Rigano is an acclaimed actor and the cohost of *The Wiseguy Show* on Sirius Satellite Radio and has appeared in many movies, usually playing a gangster, including *Johnny Slade's Greatest Hits, Coffee and Cigarettes, Analyze This, This Thing of Ours, Italian Lessons,* and *Casino,* among others.

Joan Rivers (www.joanrivers.com) is an internationally known comedian and media personality who has appeared on every major talk show including *The Tonight Show Starring Johnny Carson,* her own talk show on FOX, *Late Show Starring Joan Rivers,* the daytime talk show *The Joan Rivers Show,* and a long-running daytime talk show *Look Up.* Rivers is also known as the host of E! Entertainment Television's fashion reviews and, along with her daughter Melissa, as host of E!'s live preshow commentary for the Academy Awards, Golden Globe Awards, and Emmy Awards.

Todd Robbins (www.toddrobins.com) is a world-class magician. Besides creating and starring in the off-Broadway hit *Carnival Knowledge,* he has logged more than 100 appearances on television, including multiple appearances on *The Late Show with David Letterman, The Tonight Show with Jay Leno,* and *Late Night with Conan O'Brien,* as well as the NBC special *Extreme Variety.*

Peaches Rodriguez (www.gopeaches.com) is a stand-up comedian and former break dancer who has done three USO tours of duty, including traveling to five countries in the Middle East: Afghanistan, Pakistan, Quatar, Saudi Arabia, and Oman.

Gregg Rogell (www.myspace.com/greggrogell) is a stand-up comedian and actor who appeared in the 2005 film *The Aristocrats,* his own Comedy Central special, and *The Nanny.* He has also appeared on *The Tonight Show with Jay Leno.*

Freddie Roman is the dean of the New York Friars Club and a comedian who has headlined at many of the major resorts across the country, including Caesar's Palace in Las Vegas and Harrah's in Atlantic City. He was also the producer and star of *Catskills on Broadway*. Roman's television credits include *The Tonight Show Starring Johnny Carson*, his own special, *The Big Room* for MTV's Ha! TV Comedy Network, and *Comedy Central Presents: The New York Friars Club Roasts of Hugh Hefner, Chevy Chase, Rob Reiner*, and *Drew Carey*.

Dave Rosner (www.daverosner.com) is a former U.S. Marine veteran and stand-up comic who has performed all over the United States and Australia. His credits include appearing several times as a political and military commentator on the Comcast Network, numerous television and film appearances in Australia, and *The Man Show* on Comedy Central, where he was a contributing writer.

Jeffrey Ross (www.jeffreyross.com) is a nationally known stand-up comic-actor known for his performances at celebrity roasts like Hugh Hefner, Pamela Anderson, Donald Trump, Jerry Stiller, Drew Carey, and Shaquille O'Neal. His television credits include *The Late Show with David Letterman*, *The Tonight Show with Jay Leno*, *Jimmy Kimmel Live*, *Late Night with Conan O'Brien*, *Last Call with Carson Daly*, ABC's *The View*, and HBO's *Real Time with Bill Maher* and *Six Feet Under*, and Showtime's *Weeds*. His film credits include the Farrelley brothers' *Stuck on You*, Paul Weitz's *American Dreamz*, and the critically acclaimed comedy *The Aristocrats*.

Steve Rossi performs as part of the comedy team Allen & Rossi.

Tony Ray Rossi is an actor best known for his portrayal of Fabian "Febby" Petrulio on *The Sopranos*. He also has numerous television and film credits including *Donnie Brascoe*, *Law & Order*, *Find Me Guilty*, *Mail Order Bride*, *Analyze This*, and many others.

Roz is a stand-up comedian who was has been featured on NBC's *Last Comic Standing* in addition to having been seen in Jamie Foxx's *Laffapalooza 2006*, BET's *Comic View 2005*, VH1's *Sixteen*

Candles Reunion and *From A to Z*, as well as Comedy Central's *Premium Blend*.

Gianni Russo (www.giannirusso.semkor.com) is a veteran film actor best known for his portrayal of Carlo Rizzo in *The Godfather*. His television credits include *The Rockford Files* and *Kojak*, as well as more than forty films including *The Freshman, Rush Hour, Any Given Sunday* and *Seabiscuit*. Most recently, he filmed a reality show called *Day in the Life Of*.

Aleta St. James (www.aletasaintjames.com) is a New Age movement energy healer, author, lecturer, and former actress who is legendary for becoming a mother for the first time at age fifty-seven. St. James has been featured on the cover of *New York Magazine* and in the *New York Times* and *People, Elle, Allure, W Magazine, Harpers Bazaar,* and *Shape* magazines. She has appeared on hundreds of television and radio programs, including NBC's the *Today* show and *Dateline,* ABC's *Good Morning America,* and CNN. She has written a monthly column in *American Health and Fitness,* has consulted for the Equinox Health Clubs, and is on the board of Dr. Vagnini's Longevity Centers in New York. She has recently opened an antiaging spa called the Goddess Repair Shop in Manhattan.

George Sarris (www.sarris.net) is the founder and president of Sarris Productions, an award-winning New York City–based production company that specializes in live events such as the New York City Underground Comedy Festival, which he also created.

Silver Saundors-Friedman is the cofounder of the legendary Improv Comedy Club. She lives in New York.

Bill Scheft is the former head writer for both NBC's *Late Show with David Letterman* and CBS's *Late Show with David Letterman.* He currently writes a column for Sports Illustrated called "The Show" and is the author of *Time Won't Let Me, The Best of the Show,* and *The Ringer.* He has also contributed articles and essays to publications such as *TV Guide, Talk Slate, and Modern Humorist.*

Sparky Schneider (www.sparkysparky.com *and* www.myspace. com) is a nationally known stand-up comic who regularly performs in New York and at comedy clubs around the country.

Carol Scibelli (www.poorwidowme.blogspot.com) is an award-winning comedy writer, founding member of Manhattan Playwrights, Inc., frequent contributor to *Newsday,* and proud member of the New York Friars Club.

Marvin Scott is a seven-time Emmy Award–winning broadcast journalist who is the senior correspondent for WPIX-TV in New York.

Steven Scott (www.stevenscott.tv) is a stand-up comedian-impressionist who regularly appears at comedy clubs in New York and major venues all around the country. His television credits include the VH1 series *I Love the '90s,* and he has appeared on NBC, FOX, Comedy Central, MTV, and CBS's *Star Search,* where he was a semifinalist.

Paul Shaffer is an award-winning musician-actor who has been David Letterman's musical director and sidekick since 1985. His other television credits include *Saturday Night Live* and the CBS comedy series *A Year at the Top.* He also served as the musical director for John Belushi and Dan Aykroyd, who performed as the Blues Brothers. His film credits include *This is Spinal Tap, Gilda Live, Scrooged,* and *Look Who's Talking Too.*

Rick Shapiro (www.rickshapiro.net) is a nationally known stand-up comedian and actor who co-starred as Jerry in the HBO series *Lucky Louie.* His other credits include *Law & Order* and such films as *Pootie Tang, Tomorrow Night, Pure Danger,* and *True Love.*

Tom Shillue is a stand-up comedian and comedy writer who has appeared on *Late Night with Conan O'Brien*, NBC's *Late Friday*, and *The Daily Show with Jon Stewart*. Voted the top comic in New York by *Backstage Magazine*, he has also been featured in hundreds of commercials for products such as Snickers, Verizon, Audi, and Lay's Potato Chips, among others.

John "Goumba Johnny" Sialiano (www.goumbajohnny.com) is a nationally known radio personality, comedian and writer who is currently the co-host of the *Goumba Johnny and Hollywood Hamilton Show* on WKTU radio in New York. In addition to having also appeared on various television shows, including *Growing Up Gotti*, *The Weakest Link*, *The Montel Williams Show*, and *Tough Crowd with Colin Quinn*. Look for his upcoming book *So You Wanna Be a Mobster: Starting Your Own Mafia Family For Fun and Profit* in March 2008.

Howard Siegel is an entertainment attorney based in New York.

Tony Sirico is a veteran television and film actor who currently plays Paulie "Walnuts" Gualtieri on *The Sopranos*. He has appeared in over thirty-six films including *The Godfather*, *Goodfellas*, *Gotti*, *Mob Queen*, *Deconstructing Harry*, *Mighty Aphrodite*, and *Bullets over Broadway*, among others. In addition, he has appeared as himself on *The Tony Danza Show*, *Late Night with Conan O'Brien*, *The Best of the Insult Comic Dog*, *The Late Show with David Letterman*, and the Sixth Annual Screen Actors Guild Awards.

Laura Slutsky is the president and CEO of PeopleFinders, an award-winning commercial documentary company in New York. She is also a professional comedian and cabaret singer and has written many articles on women in advertising.

Sherrod Small (www.sherrodsmall.com) is a nationally known stand-up comedian and actor who currently hosts *Best Week Ever* on VH1. His other credits include appearances on *The Chris Rock Show* on HBO and *Tough Crowd with Colin Quinn* on Comedy Central, among others.

Robert Smigel is a stand-up comedian and performer best known for his *Saturday Night Live* "TV Funhouse" cartoon shorts and as the puppeteer behind Triumph, the Insult Comic Dog.

Eddie Sommerfield was an agent in the personal appearance department of the William Morris Agency for more than twenty years. During that time his clients have included Rodney Dangerfield, Joan Rivers, Robert Klein, Alan Sherman, Jackie Mason, Corbett Monica, David Brenner and many others.

Tammy Faye Starlight (www.tammyfayestarlight.com) is a New York-based comedian and singer.

Joe Starr (www.myspace.com/thebigjoestarr) is a nationally known touring comedian and actor who has appeared on Comedy Central's *Premium Blend*. His film credits include *World Trade Center* and the independent film *Merry Little Christmas*.

Evan Steinberg (www.steinbergtalent.com) is the co-owner of Steinberg Talent Managment Group in New York.

Stewie Stone is an internationally known stand-up comic who has opened for Paul Anka, Frankie Valli, the Village People, Shirley Bassey, Roberta Flack, Gladys Knight and the Pips, the Temptations, and the Four Tops. He has performed in the big rooms of Las Vegas, Madison Square Garden, Carnegie Hall, Atlantic City, and all across the country and overseas.

Elaine Stritch is a legendary performer of stage and screen who recently appeared in a one-woman Broadway show, *Elaine Stritch At Liberty*, which won both a Tony and an Emmy Award.

Ivy Supersonic (www.ivysupersonic.com) is a hat designer, media personality, and socialite who has designed hats for Pamela Anderson, Snoop Dogg, Carmen Electra, among many others. She has been featured on VH-1, Wild On E!, Fashion Television, CNN, and numerous other networks and shows.

D. F. Sweedler is a stand-up comedian-writer who regularly performs at the Comic Strip in New York, where he also teaches a course in comedy performing. In addition, he is a former monologue writer for David Letterman.

Wil Sylvince is a stand-up comedian-writer who tours the country and has also appeared on BET and Comedy Central and is the coproducer of NBC's *Comedy Short Cuts*.

Brad Trackman (www.bradtrackman.com) is a weekend regular at the Comic Strip Live, Carolines on Broadway, the Comedy Cellar, Stand Up New York, and Gotham Comedy Club. He is a graduate of the American Academy of Dramatic Arts, and his television credits include NBC's *Later* and *Friday Night*, CBS's *Star Search*, Comedy Central's *Heroes of Jewish Comedy*, *New Joke City* hosted by Robert Klein, and ABC's NY *Comedy Festival Special*.

Fred Travalena (www.fredtravalena.com) is a comedian, impressionist, actor, and singer. His impersonations of highly visible public figures have earned him the nickname "the Man of a Thousand Faces." He has appeared on many top television talk shows such as *The Late Show with David Letterman*, *The Tonight Show with Jay Leno*, *Larry King Live*, and *Regis and Kathie Lee*.

Andy Tsagaris (www.andytsagaris.com) is a stand-up comedian who appears regularly at comedy clubs in New York and throughout the country. His film and television credits include *The New*

Yorker Talkshow, *Where God Left His Shoes*, and NBC's *Convictions*.

Eha Urbsalu (www.ehamusic.com) is an international singing star and a former Miss Estonia, where she grew up. She performs at major venues in this country and around the world.

Sandra Valls (www.myspace.com/sandravalls) is the creator of *Butch Talk* and has appeared on HBO's *Latino*, Starz Network's *First Amendment Comedy*, BET's *Comic View*, and CTV's *Que Locos*.

Andy Vastola (www.andyvastola.com) is a nationally touring stand-up comedian who performs regularly at clubs in New York and around the nation. His credits include *The Late Show with David Letterman* and *Star Search*.

Jim Vern (www.cam1vid.com) is a New York-based comedy videographer and comedy producer who has taped shows at all of New York's major comedy venues, including Caroline's on Broadway, Stand-Up New York, The Comic Strip Live, Gotham Comedy Club, and The Comedy Cellar.

Vinny Vella is a television and film actor whose credits include *The Sopranos*, *Law & Order*, *Analyze That*, *Casino*, *Find Me Guilty*, *Donnie Brasco*, and *Coffee and Cigarettes*, among others.

Erik Von Broock is a nightlife impresario, club owner, and the cofounder of the V&V Energy Drink.

Rich Vos is a stand-up comic best known from the first season of the NBC reality show *Last Comic Standing*. He currently appears regularly on radio on *The Opie and Anthony Show*, and was also a regular on Comedy Central's *Tough Crowd with Colin Quinn*. In addition, he has appeared in his own Comedy Central half-hour special, ABC's *The View*, *The Rosie O'Donnell Show*, *Chappelle's Show*, and HBO's *Def Comedy Jam*.

Aesha Waks (www.aeshawaks.com) is an award-winning actress and model.

Wendel is a stand-up comic based in New York who regularly opens for Lisa Lampanelli.

Sir Ivan Wilzig (www.sirivan.com) is a nationally known singing star, philanthropist and international banker.

Buck Wolf is an internet journalist who writes "The Wolf Files" for ABC News.com.

Walter Yetnikoff is the former president of CBS Records and a music industry legend who was a major influence in the careers of artists such as Michael Jackson, Bruce Springsteen, Billy Joel, Barbra Streisand, and Leonard Bernstein. He is also the author of *Howling at the Moon.*

Rick Younger (www.rickyounger.com) is a multi-talented actor, comedian and singer whose credits include BET's *Comic View* and *Teen Summit*, FOX's *30 Seconds to Fame*, *It's Showtime at the Apollo*, and NBC's *Last Comic Standing.*

Dr. Victoria (Dr. Z) Zdrok (www.sexysexpert.com) is a world renowned media personality, dating coach and relationship advisor. Formerly a *Playboy* Playmate and *Penthouse Pet of the Year*, she currently writes a monthly sex and love advice column for *Penthouse* and has authored several books on love, sex and dating. She is also the host of her own talk show, *The Sex Connection*, on Sirius Satellite Radio.

Alan Zweibel was one of the original writers on *Saturday Night Live* and has won numerous Emmy and Writers Guild awards for his work in television, which also includes *It's Gary Shandling's*

Show, PBS's *Great Performances*, and *Curb Your Enthusiasm*. His theater credits include *Bunny Bunny: Gilda Radner—A Sort of Romantic Comedy*, Billy Crystal's one-man Broadway show *700 Sundays*, and Martin Short's *Fame Becomes Me*. He is the author of the novel *The Other Shulman*, for which he won the Thurber Prize.

Acknowledgments

Despite the content and theme of this book, it was really a labor of love for me to write and compile. It would probably have been more accurate to have named it *So If I Know All These People, How Come I'm Not Famous?* But maybe that will be my next book.

That being said, for whatever reason, I have earned a reputation as a roast writer and writing *schmutz* (dirty stuff) for very famous people. God seems to have blessed me with a filthy mind, and it was always fun writing those kind of jokes, and even better actually hearing big stars verbalize them.

I want to thank Tripp Whetsell for making this all happen; my editor Gary Goldstein, for his support, good sense of humor, and friendship; Michaela Hamilton, for giving her okay to the project; and my agent Peter Rubie. Also, I want to thank all the people who agreed to be in this book, and even the few who turned me down. (They all did it in the nicest way. No one said, "Fuck you, Jeffrey, and don't ever call me again!")

I want to thank some of the people who asked me to write this *schmutz* over the years. Special thanks to Jean-Pierre Trebot, the director of the Friars Club, Michael Caputo, the assistant director, and those who came before them, such as Walter Goldstein, Buddy Howe, Dave Tebett, and the legendary Bob Saks. I want to thank Dick Capri for giving me my start and for being the first comedian to ever use my jokes onstage. (And this is how I repay him!)

Acknowledgments

I want to thank Freddie Roman, the esteemed dean of the Friars Club, for also being one of the first to let me write for him. I also want to thank Freddie for not hating me for the time I got him out of bed to rehearse for a roast, only to discover that I had left the material at home.

Special thanks to others who helped me and mentored me along the way, some of whom may not even remember doing so, but who I'll never forget! People such as Alan Zweibel; David Jonas; Jack Rollins; Charlie Joffe; Woody Allen; Herb Sargent; Bill Persky; Judy McGrath, who hired me to write *The Friday Night Video Fights* on MTV; Phil Hartman, for his friendship and support and for allowing me to create things for him; Frank Chindamo (mostly for laughing very loud at everything I ever wrote); Jackie Mason, for his friendship, support, and confidence; Jyll Rosenfeld, who also smiled at a couple of things I wrote; and finally Paul Provenza of *The Aristocrats*, who has known me since my other life and whose tooth I actually fixed when he chipped it onstage one night. (I think that's why he agreed to write the foreword.)

I want to thank my two beautiful daughters, Elizabeth and Kathryn, who I fervently hope will never see this book; my mom, for putting up with the insanity and not having me put away; and my dad, who gave me my sense of humor and never took it back.

And thanks to Nana Fay, my dear maternal grandmother, who let me smear cream cheese on her ankles and spoke in a phony Jewish accent for a film I was doing, and to Nana Kitty, my fraternal grandmother, for letting me squeeze corn on her eyeglasses and never getting angry.

A special thanks to the legendary Jan Murray, who left us two weeks after I called him to ask him about using some of the lines I wrote for him back in 1981. And like the trooper he was, he got on the phone to speak to me, even though he had just gotten out of the hospital, and it was very hard for him to speak. Rest in peace, Jan.

And a very special thank you to my sponsor in the Friars Club, and a very dear friend and mentor, the legendary Milton Berle, the greatest roast master of all time, who helped me in so many ways.

Even after all the years I knew him as a friend, I could never believe it when I was speaking to him on the phone. I'd be in the middle of speaking to him, and all of a sudden I'd think to myself, "Holy shit, I'm speaking to Milton Berle."

Thanks, Milton, for having the biggest *schvontz* in the business so I could write jokes about it and get to meet and befriend you. I think I can honestly say, it's only fitting and proper, which is more than I could say for Youngman's suit (your line!), your *schlong* changed my life!

—

Three of my classic Milton Berle jokes
If Berle's cock had a blond wig, it could pass for Paul Williams.

Milton would have been here tonight, but he was fucking this chick in his hotel room, and on his way over to the bed, he accidentally tripped and pole-vaulted out the window.

Milton was a very generous man. He was so generous, he once invited me and my family out on his cock for the weekend.

—Jeffrey L. Gurian

Among the many good fortunes I've been lucky enough to have had bestowed upon me as an author, my biggest are my editor Gary Goldstein and my agent Peter Rubie, who are two of the most brilliant, generous, and supportive men in the world of book publishing, bar none, who keep my world sane and my days occupied. Also, thanks to my partner, Jeffrey L. Gurian, a man I consider one of my best friends in the world, not to mention a brilliant comedy writer without whom this book would not have been possible. Thanks, also, to all of my wonderful family and friends—especially Gus Weill, for being a mentor and surrogate father figure sent down from the heavens and who has been in my life forever, it seems, even though we only met recently. And a special thank you to my beloved friend, Sharon Klein, for being the beautiful person she is inside and out, and to our precious Malteses, Jack and Oliver.

—Tripp Whetsell